HOMETOWN TALES
LANCASHIRE

HOMETOWN TALES is a series of books pairing exciting new voices with some of the most talented and important authors at work today. Each of the writers has contributed an original tale on the theme of hometown, exploring places and communities in the UK where they have lived or think of as home.

Some of the tales are fiction and some are narrative non-fiction – they are all powerful, fascinating and moving, and aim to celebrate regional diversity and explore the meaning of home.

HOMETOWN TALES
LANCASHIRE

JENN ASHWORTH
BENJAMIN WEBSTER

WEIDENFELD & NICOLSON

First published in Great Britain in 2018 by Weidenfeld & Nicolson
an imprint of The Orion Publishing Group Ltd
Carmelite House, 50 Victoria Embankment
London EC4Y 0DZ

An Hachette UK Company

1 3 5 7 9 10 8 6 4 2

After the Funeral, the Crawl © Jenn Ashworth 2018
JUDAS! © Benjamin Webster 2018

A CIP catalogue record for this book is available from the British Library.

ISBN (Hardback) 978 1 4746 0823 7
ISBN (eBook) 978 1 4746 0824 4

Typeset at The Spartan Press Ltd,
Lymington, Hants

Printed and bound in Great Britain by Clays Ltd, Elcograf, S.p.A

www.orionbooks.co.uk

CONTENTS

After the Funeral, the Crawl

Jenn Ashworth

JENN ASHWORTH was born in 1982 in Preston. She studied English at Cambridge and since then has gained an MA from Manchester University, trained as a librarian and run a prison library in Lancashire. She now lectures in Creative Writing at the University of Lancaster. Her first novel, *A Kind of Intimacy*, was published in 2009 and won a Betty Trask Award. Her second, *Cold Light*, was published by Sceptre in 2011 and she was chosen by BBC's The Culture Show as one of the twelve Best New British Novelists. Her most recent novels are *The Friday Gospels* and *Fell*. She lives in Lancaster.

For my friend Sarah F., because of all
our conversations about endings

THE OLD VIC, FISHERGATE HILL

THEY MISSED THE last London train and bickered for a while on the platform about whose fault it was, though without much enthusiasm. She suggested they find a pub with Wi-Fi and book either a hotel or hire a car. He didn't want to, but didn't have an alternative suggestion. The nearest place was directly opposite the station, and it was having a quiz night.

'His mum's aged,' she said, once they'd found a table. She poured orange juice from a little glass bottle into her vodka.

He clocked this. Realised that if they were going to hire a car, it had already been assumed that he would be the one driving it.

'I wouldn't have recognised her if I'd bumped into her in the street,' she added, looking at him then, wanting him to respond. She had started to worry lately – since he had begun to point it out – that she

5

talked too much, or too loudly, or too quickly. Some days she thought it wasn't that she was too much, it was that he wasn't enough. She silently counted to ten to give him time to say something. She knew he didn't want to be in the pub.

He nodded at her and took a sip from his pint, then looked away, at the posters for special offers on bottled beer that were stuck all over the pub walls. There was a machine in the corner that looked like one of the old-fashioned gumball machines, but this one dispensed nuts. Even as his eyes wandered around the pub, he felt her eyes on him, her gaze like the tiny pinpricks of a biting insect. What she wanted was unclear to him. This pub wasn't especially familiar to either of them. They were out of sorts, that's all. Home, but not at home. There was no memory he could dredge up of the last time he was here, either with her or by himself, no piece of nostalgia he could give to her to get the conversation going.

'She'll have been upset,' he said, finally. 'She looked upset.'

She eagerly – gratefully – took this up.

'Oh God, yes. I mean, it was a shock, wasn't it? People say if it was expected. If it was cancer. They talk about long illnesses and battles and courage and whatnot. I didn't hear anything like that. It must have been sudden. She will have been in shock.'

She pictured the woman – only half familiar to her from years past – sitting at the head of the table at the wake in the church hall, as if at a wedding, being brought cups of tea and tissues and being attended to by two teenagers in suits who must have been nephews. The woman – not old, but crumpled – sat there with her tea, not talking, only nodding and accepting the condolences of those who stopped to talk to her for a moment or two. She wasn't really in the room at all. Above her there were cheaply printed posters for next week's Psychic Night Blu-Tacked to the window. Word Art.

'Maybe it was his heart,' he said, still considering the nut machine. Roasted peanuts, cashews and pistachios. Probably been quietly festering for months. He wasn't there yet, but he was rapidly approaching the age when his GP would start questioning him about his fry-ups and cigarettes and asking him to count and report on his weekly units when he'd only turned up at the surgery to get a verruca looked at. The waistband of his suit trousers was digging into his gut and it was impossible to sit up straight and be comfortable in them. He tried to feel his heart; to become aware of it beating steadily in his chest. He looked away from the nuts and at her, and yes, she was still staring at him.

'Sudden can mean heart, can't it?' he said.

'They'd have said if it was his heart, wouldn't they? Somebody would have said. He was too young for that.'

'Didn't anyone say?'

'I didn't ask. There wasn't anybody I knew well enough.'

The quiz was going on around them. He worried that they were too conspicuous, he in his second-best suit and she in her black dress, sitting together in a corner when the rest of the pub had split into rowdy groups noisily conferring and scribbling their answers onto sheets of paper. They weren't exactly being stared at, but he felt like a sore thumb all the same. He should have suggested something else. A coach, perhaps.

The quizmaster was sitting at the end of the bar shouting his questions into a microphone, which roared and whistled with feedback. The next question was about the Bible.

'Amen,' he said.

'What?' She thought he was agreeing with her

8

about not knowing anyone at the funeral. He twitched his head towards the bar.

'The last word in the New Testament. Amen.'

'Amazing. We should have entered,' she said, and marvelled at how sarcastic she could sound without meaning to. 'Did you talk to his mother?'

'Only to say hello. To say it was a lovely service and we were sorry. She didn't know me.' He meant it in the sense of 'remember' – but there was that too, that sense of being unknown, of being on the outside of things, that he'd felt, and hadn't expected.

'I hate this,' she said, fidgeting. 'I want to go home. Back. Are there really no trains?'

They had been through this already – the last one, the one they were supposed to be on – had left without them at nine. He took out his phone and started looking for car hires. The Wi-Fi in the pub stuttered and his browser was slow to connect. Was it expensive to hire a car at short notice?

He felt a moment of panic – that sense of being stuck, of being moored somewhere, without help. And this was his home. He hadn't told his mother he was coming back today. As far as he knew, neither had she told her father. It was supposed to be just a day visit.

'We might have to stay. Should we phone your dad?' he asked, knowing already what her answer would be. 'I know it's not ideal, but—'

She snorted, not needing to tell him that, according to her, the possibility of either of them phoning – or even worse – turning up – at their parents' houses and asking for a bed for the night was out of the question. No need for the rigmarole of a return to the single beds with faded duvet covers from childhood, the hastily put together welcome, the questions about work petering out until someone – thank God – put the television on. They'd make a proper visit at Christmas, which wasn't too far away.

'He's not that bad,' he said. Yes, there was Brexit, and his opinions about – well, most things – but everyone's parents were like that, weren't they? Didn't everyone have a whole list of things they didn't speak to their mum and dad about? Sharp edges they became willing to work around, just for the sake of a pleasant evening? If he said that, she'd call him a name. Sell-out, turncoat. Something like that.

'I'm not staying there,' she said. And that was that.

'My mother?' he glanced at his watch. Getting a bit too late to phone her now. He imagined her, impossibly elderly (he'd been a late, unexpected baby – a possibly unwanted one, he always wondered – mistaken for the menopause), hunched before her crossword book with a flask of tea. She only boiled the kettle once in the evening. He didn't know which way she'd voted. She probably hadn't voted at all. 'We could get a taxi. She'd be happy to see us,' he said.

And she would. She'd tut and bring stew out of the freezer and, in the morning, put him to work, clearing the gutters or moving things around in the loft, and make good-natured but not entirely innocent comments about them not coming home for Christmas last year, and about grandchildren, and about how careers and money weren't everything, you know. How he had no business getting above himself. Forgetting where he came from.

For himself, he could enjoy all that. Could experience it as a variety of love: the chilly, taciturn variety that his mother specialised in, and which had, despite anything, managed to nourish him well. But his girl-friend – who was swilling the ice about in the bottom of her glass impatiently – would turn his mother's meaningful glance at her abdomen into a fully fledged argument, and he hadn't the heart to mediate between them again.

'A car or a hotel. Just find us one or the other, would you?' she said. She was, he knew, of the opinion that any functioning human being grew out of having parents, the way they grew out of their childhood bedroom. Maybe she was right. 'I'm going to the bar.'

He gave her a twenty from his wallet and watched her as she went. He observed the way the belt of her coat was twisted through its belt loops and looked untidy. She wouldn't like that. He decided not to mention it.

There was a bit of a queue – they were between quiz rounds and everybody wanted a drink – so while she waited he stepped outside to smoke a cigarette.

It wasn't completely dark yet. The sky was smudged yellow, as it always is in cities, though it was still hard to think of this place as a city, especially after spending over a decade living in a proper one. A bus slowed and pulled up a little way down the road in front of a hairdresser's that used to be an enormous shoe shop called Tommy Balls. It decanted a group of young women, dressed up, hair piled high. They were laughing about something. Him? He averted his eyes. It wasn't that he particularly wanted to look and had to restrain himself, but because to be caught looking would be humiliating. The arrogance of it.

His mother – sharply present in his mind now – would take him once a year to that shoe shop – because it was cheap – and get him school shoes and black pumps for PE. The kids in his class could always tell who'd been to Balls and not Clarks, because Tommy Balls used to put string through the back of the shoes and hang them up in pairs, and the little hole the string left in the back of the shoe never went away.

He glanced again at the people disembarking from the bus. Imagining his mother being there – God knows why she would be, but stranger things have happened – and catching sight of him waiting here. Back home, and without a word of warning to her. Of course she'd take it personally.

He took his phone out again and carried on looking for car hires. She could drink his beer, and he'd be all right to drive, and then she'd sleep all the way back on two double vodkas and his second Heineken. It would make her feel better, to be on her way out of here. And that would result in a more peaceful evening. And hiring a car wouldn't be that expensive: probably only a little more than a last-minute hotel booking. They should have done that in the first place. But despite all his searching, the only car-hire place he could find was right out of town, and it closed at six. They were stuck.

He stepped towards the kerb to throw the end of his cigarette – smoked right down to the filter – into the drain, and saw the pouches under his eyes in his reflection in another bus window: just a flash, as it passed, but it was enough.

She waited for him inside, sitting alone at the table with his beer and her vodka and orange juice. She was hungry. There was food at the wake – just little things passed around on trays – but it hadn't felt right to sit herself down on a folding chair and stuff her face, and she didn't know anyone else to speak to, and everyone else seemed to know each other and not who they were, so it had been awkward, and she'd started to wonder if the wake was for closer friends and family only, and not them, who were now only visitors to their hometown. Guests. And barely invited. She'd eaten nothing in the end, only drunk two cups of warmish tea. Her feet hurt.

She was trying to accept that they were stuck here for the night. That the car-hire idea was a non-starter. A hotel, then. They could make the best out of this.

It would be nice, for example, if he'd come back in after his fag and say that, seeing as they were stuck here, they might as well find a restaurant and treat themselves to a slap-up meal. It might not be too late for that if they got on with it. A bottle of something fizzy in a silver bucket. And a hotel. When was the last time they had . . . ? They could pretend it was their anniversary. Leave the television off. Neither of them had brought their laptops, so there'd be no distractions.

He used to put his hands into her hair when he kissed her. Maybe, away from home, out of his usual routine, he'd think to do that again. She'd let him, if he started it. He'd have to start it. But she wouldn't complain about the smell of his cigarettes. She didn't have anything nice to wear for bed and neither of them had toothbrushes, but maybe they'd take a shower together. If he suggested that, or just took her hand and pulled her into the bathroom, she would say yes. She would go along with it. It had been a long time.

'All the car hires are shut,' he said, as he slid awkwardly back into his seat. He picked up his fresh pint and took a long drink from it. 'I keep wondering if he did it himself.'

She frowned. 'It won't have been anything like that,' she said.

There was something in her tone – some kind of annoyance or irritation that interested him. He must play this carefully. Asking what the matter was would only open the floodgates – and in public, with nowhere else to go – so he watched the level in her glass sinking rapidly and opted instead for a more oblique approach.

'Did you google him?'

'What? No.'

'There might have been something online somewhere. They always put it in the paper when someone goes off the top of the bus station.'

'Don't. That's nasty.'

He wiped his top lip. 'It's true though. I read about it somewhere. Our hometown is the suicide capital of the country, apparently. And we have the most pubs.'

'That's rubbish.'

She was offended, and it was more than just her sense of decency outraged by his curiosity. This was more personal than that. He noted it.

'I'm just saying. If that's what he'd done – if he'd jumped – then they'd have put it in the paper.'

'I wish they wouldn't. It's horrible. They should put netting up.'

It was Si's younger brother – Mark, he was called – who had found her on Facebook and had sent a message during the night two weeks ago. He apologised for the medium (that was the strangest thing – the formality of that – and coming from a man they could both only remember as a peripheral, mildly irritating fifteen-year-old with a bleach-blond ponytail and a tattered, second-hand Greenday T-shirt) but his elder brother Simon had died, and he was doing the rounds, calling and contacting all of his old friends – 'the gang' – and letting them know about the arrangements for the funeral. It would be nice, he'd said, especially for his mother, if they could come and represent that part of his life. He hadn't used the word died. He'd said, 'passed away. Very unexpected. We're all wrecked.'

So they'd come as representatives of their late teen years, both of them telling the other they expected to be reunited with old friends, and to have a bit of a knees-up afterwards, and find out what everyone had been doing. To be welcomed back. They said this quietly, of course – and only between themselves.

Anything else would have been crass. In private though, each of them thought differently. He had been coldly neutral, tilting towards the curious – wanting to see what she would do. And she was almost dreading it. Still, together, they had persisted in quietly looking forward to the party.

But it turned out the gang really had dispersed. The two of them had gone first – to study in London, then stayed for work. They lived in an ex-council flat in Lewisham – both in publishing (he in sales, she in publicity – they had an agreement never to talk shop at the dinner table, and instead ate side by side on the sofa, catching up on whatever Netflix series they'd committed to that month). They were settled. No plans to come back.

Mark had sent more Facebook messages over the next week to fill them in on where the others had gone. Sarah, who they only vaguely remembered, had finished her goth phase and was doing something with a charity in China, and couldn't come such a long way on short notice. Helen was with her wife teaching something or other at a Christian university in Idaho, improbably, and Mark's Facebook message to her had remained unread. The rest were scattered, didn't use social media, or couldn't otherwise be found. The ones that could had their own excuses. Children, mainly, who couldn't travel, or be taken out of school, or found babysitters for.

'Everyone's got babies now,' Mark had written.

She sent a message asking Mark if there was anywhere Si would have wanted her to donate to in his memory. That would have been a clue. It was the polite way to ask. If Mark had asked for money for a specific organisation – a hospice, or the British Heart Foundation, or something else – it would have cleared it up. But there was no named place for donations and so the trail went cold. It wasn't as if you could just come out and ask, no matter how close you'd once been.

'They wouldn't have had a wake if he'd have done it himself. They don't have wakes after suicides,' he said.

'Who told you that?'

It wasn't like she wanted it to be a suicide. Sometimes she thought she disagreed with him just for the sake of it – just because it seemed to snag him into a conversation, and stopped him wandering away, or going within himself, the way he always did these days. She knew if she raised this with him, he'd say he only withdrew because she was argumentative, and there was no pleasing her, and round they'd go. It was an argument they hadn't quite given up having yet. The repetitiveness of it, and the way it seemed to pin her into the stereotype of a needy, nagging wife (they weren't married, though it had been nearly twenty years now – imagine that) didn't stop her doing it.

He shrugged, and if there was a point, conceded it immediately, because the conversation didn't matter. She didn't matter.

She wanted to put the palms of her hands on the table and lean forward and make him look at her properly and ask him, in a low and forceful voice, exactly what his problem was. Tell him she wasn't keeping him prisoner, and he could go and get a taxi all the way to Lewisham if he wanted to. Tell him that at the very least he could practise some basic civility and look at her when he was speaking to her. But she didn't. She bit the inside of her cheek and waited for him to say something. *Your turn.*

'I don't suppose there'll be a Premier Inn here,' he said. 'My mum would—'

'There is,' she held up her phone. 'It's new. Newish. New to us. We can walk. I'll book us a room now. And breakfast.'

'The train in the morning will be a fortune.'

'Yes, probably.'

She earned slightly more and he took this 'probably' to be her way of pointing that out – that of the two of them, she was the one who had decent credit and the space on the card to book two peak-time last-minute tickets from Preston down to London with hardly a second thought.

'It was funny, seeing Mark – wasn't it? I hardly remember him. Always thought of him as a baby,' she said. She busied herself with her phone, swiping and sighing when the browser was too slow to respond.

'Two years younger is a lot when you're seventeen, I suppose. Nothing at all now.'

'Did you ask him what he was doing? Is he still here?'

'He's at that call centre. Not with his mum any more, but a house near the park.'

'Fucking hell.'

'I bet his place is bigger than ours.'

She didn't respond to this. She was thinking about Mark – his suit slightly too small for him, his hair cut short (it had probably been short for years: he'd be in his thirties too, only a couple of years behind them),

21

being the man of the house and directing people into their seats for the funeral.

She'd seen him outside the church hall as they'd left, leaning against the wall and smoking. Gone over and told him how lovely the service was and how nice it had been to be invited. How much it meant to them to be remembered as part of Si's life. He hadn't been funny with her. Hadn't given any clue that he was secretly holding her responsible. But what was normal, at funerals? She'd been searching for an anecdote about Si to relay to him – something funny, that might have cheered him up a bit and cemented Si's place in her personal history, and so her place at this funeral, where, after all, she did not belong, but she could come up with nothing except an invitation.

'You'll have to stay in touch,' she'd said. It was the kind of thing you did say. 'Come and stay with us the next time you're in London.'

He'd looked at her strangely. 'I'm not, very often.'

'Right. Well. If you ever are,' she ploughed on, while he finished his cigarette and the taxi arrived. 'For a show. Or a meeting. You know. A gig.' Did he like music? Did people still call them gigs? She couldn't remember. 'We don't have a spare room. But a sofa bed. You could email us. It would be great to get together. To talk about Si. Old memories. That sort of thing.' He was frowning at her now, but she couldn't stop talking. She had leaned forward and awkwardly hugged him, grazing one of her knuckles on the wall he was leaning against, and told him again that it had been a lovely service, and then fled into the taxi where her boyfriend was already waiting.

'What was all that about?' he'd said as she got in, only having seen her launch herself at Mark, and she hadn't answered but made herself busy, fastening her seatbelt and advising the taxi driver of the route she wanted him to take, and after that they'd sat together in silence, not wanting to unpick the funeral in front of the driver, until the car stopped at the station.

'I think we've lost our accents,' was the only thing she'd said, as they dragged their bags across the platform, knowing already that the train departing was theirs. 'He sounded . . . I don't know, really – broad.'

They were used to this: this speculation on dialect and accent and whether they should start saying 'baaaahth' because insisting it was called a 'bath' after living amongst those who used long vowels for ten years was tantamount to attention seeking – to playing the Professional Northerner, which he was, very often, when drunk. When they'd first moved down,

23

he'd held entire bars full of people who couldn't hear the difference between a Preston and a Bolton accent captive with his terrible Peter Kay impression, and sometimes he still did. It wasn't entirely cruel.

'We haven't. We sound just the same. We're just not used to hearing them from other people. We've not been at home for ages, have we? Over a year?'

She registered him calling the city 'home', and didn't like it, but the train really had gone and they had other things to deal with.

'Do you think Si was bored? Still here, after all this time?' he asked. They'd finished the second round of drinks.

'I wouldn't know,' she said. 'I would be.'

'I know you would be,' he said, thinking of the student union competition in the first reading week of their first term at uni: some challenge to hitchhike as far away from campus as possible in three days on a forty-quid budget. She'd aced it, of course, getting to Prague and sending a picture of herself back to him drinking foamy beer in half-litre glasses with a bunch of people – some of them men – who he didn't know. She'd won the competition, but winning hadn't cured her: this urge to speed away from the place where she'd started from as soon as possible. He wanted to ask her about that. Ask her if she's slept with a truck driver, or kissed any of the boys in the picture she'd sent. But she'd only laugh at him.

'He'd started meditating,' he said. 'Mark told me. He was in some group. At it all the time. Morning and night.'

'It doesn't sound like him. All that sitting still with your eyes closed. Wasn't he some kind of speed demon? Wouldn't he have got bored?'

The past tense was ambiguous here. Unclear, he thought, if she was referring to recent dead Simon, or late-teens Simon, who had been saving up for a motorbike as the rest of them were planning for uni.

He shrugged. 'People who meditate don't get bored.'

He meant it as a joke, but she just looked at him strangely. He stood, and gathered his phone, lighter, cigarette packet. She watched him without moving. She was thinking of the picture of Simon that had been printed on the front of the Order of Service handed out at the church. In the photograph, his hair was uncut and shaggy and his T-shirt had a slogan on it in a font that was supposed to look handwritten: *I have arrived. I am home.* Something to do with meditating, wasn't it? Some Zen slogan, if Zen people were allowed to have slogans. Maybe that was a good thing. Maybe Buddhists didn't kill themselves.

'Come on,' he said.

Was he going to suggest an early bedtime, or a late dinner out somewhere? She fastened her jacket and turned her face to him hopefully.

'Let's go somewhere else.'

THE BLACK HORSE, FRIARGATE

HE LED HER up the main street, past the closed shops, and looped around, crossing the flag market diagonally in front of the big old library and museum. This was partly, he realised, a wish to see the old place: it was drizzling slightly, and most of the shop windows were shuttered up – charity shops, betting shops, a Mexican restaurant with music leaking out onto the street – and partly because the quickest route involved cutting through the main shopping centre, and it was closed, the metal shutters down.

'Where are we going?'

There were nearer pubs, but he wanted to go somewhere he knew.

'The Black Horse. Come on.'

They walked past McDonald's and Specsavers, and a computer game shop he could never remember the name of where Si had worked on Saturdays for a while, during his A Levels. Everything was the same, and not the same. The wide streets felt empty, but they weren't: there were other couples, and groups of friends trekking between pubs as they were, but there was no crush, no queue for the cash machine, no purposeful striding.

They reached the corner, the narrow door.

This pub, he did know. Almost expected to be greeted as a friend as he went through the door first, enjoying the way the tiles in the little vestibule and the coloured stained glass in the windows were exactly as he remembered. Tiles everywhere: intricate mosaics on the floor, and shiny green and terracotta tiles along the front of the ornate bar and halfway up the walls. William Morris wallpaper, or at least a good impression of it.

This place had always reminded him of a wheel in the way it was laid out, the bar a little stage in the round in the centre, with snugs, like elongated sitting rooms, leading off it like spokes. It was a better place, this one. More private. Nobody sitting staring at you and wondering why you weren't joining in with the quiz. And it wasn't too busy.

He went to the bar, knowing that she'd try the snug with the open fire in it first, even though he'd be too hot. Watching her in the bar mirror, he was glad when she saw it was too busy and went to the other one – the one more like a booth, with leather-covered benches built in around the walls and little round wooden tables down the middle.

The short walk in the open air had improved her mood, or perhaps it was just the vodka taking effect. He bought her a single, and when he got back to where she was sitting, she looked up at him, pleased.

'We're Facebook friends with Si. Did you know that? I'd totally forgotten.'

He hadn't expected her to bring him up again. But it would be weird not to speak about him on the day of his funeral.

'Let's have a look.'

She handed him her phone and he scrolled down Si's wall, noticing first the little red alert on her messenger icon. Seven messages. Who was she messaging? She said she never bothered with Facebook any more. That it was for needy fantasists. He carried on scrolling. Si, with thinning hair, standing on a beach somewhere in baggy shorts and a creased shirt. Si, standing next to a motorbike, his hand resting proprietorially on the seat. There were recent posts on his wall – all from people that neither of them were friends with. His page had turned into something like a guestbook at a funeral.

Just heard the news. Gutted mate. Keep on riding. RIP. XXXX

Si. Will never forget that night at Bitter Suite!! Crazy or what. All the best.

Can't believe it. Just sitting here in total shock. Total shock. God only takes the best ones, darling. X

'Do you think it was his motorbike?' he asked and handed her phone back.

She shrugged. 'Could be.'

'He never actually went anywhere on it, did he? Just round and round, last thing at night when the roads were clear.'

'We never spoke about it.'

'He told me once – God, this was years ago – we were still at uni, I think – that it was better than sex, that feeling. The journey, not the destination, something like that.'

She rolled her eyes. 'That sounds like him.'

'I can't even remember the last time we talked to him properly. Did you keep in touch with him. On Facebook?'

He was working his way around to asking obliquely about the notification icon she had allowed him to see, despite knowing what she'd say – that the messages were just spam about book launches, or self-published authors wanting free advice on promoting their work, or reminders to send good wishes to someone she met once, four years ago, at a book fair, because it was their birthday. But still, he wanted to know.

She swiped the Facebook application away and let him see that she'd put a password on her lock screen.

'I said happy birthday to him now and again. He put a picture up of himself in a Christmas jumper late last year, and I wished him a merry Christmas, and he asked if we were coming back for New Year.'

Back. She said 'back' and not 'home'. She'd not always done that, though. He tried to pinpoint when it started, but she was looking at him, waiting to say something in that way she had.

'What did you say to him?'

'I said no.'

They had argued about this. Not coming home for Christmas last year for the first time. Not even a flying visit at New Year.

'I had a drink with him when I was up here for Lila's christening at Easter. Do you remember that?'

He knew she wouldn't. Lila was his brother's daughter.

'I didn't come,' she said quickly. 'Remember. Work. She's nearly one now, isn't she?'

'Yeah. We went for a game of pool.'

'How was he?'

'He wasn't suicidal. He was normal.'

'I didn't mean that. I just meant . . . I don't know. It's hard to picture him as he is now. As he was. I keep seeing an eighteen-year-old.'

He nodded. 'You saw him last summer though, didn't you? When you were up?'

She didn't reply to this. She was still fiddling with her phone, refusing to meet his eye.

'You didn't tell me you'd been out with him when you came for Lila.'

'Why would I have? I didn't know he was going to . . .'

She shuddered then, and unfastened her jacket. Her face was flushed. 'This is horrible. We should stop talking about it.' She looked around them: the pub wasn't crowded, but there were people sitting in the snugs, standing at the bar. 'We could be sitting here with his best mate, for all we know. Small town, this.'

He nodded and prepared to change the subject, but she put her phone on the table decisively, face down.

'You saw him last, then. What did he say? When you were playing pool?'

'Nothing much. It was just small talk. Banter. You'd have hated it.'

Banter. She didn't think he'd ever used that word before. She tried to imagine him bantering, and couldn't.

'He mentioned a girlfriend,' he said, as if he'd only just remembered. 'Someone he'd met through his work. You remember he was at that music shop, next to the Fox and Grapes?'

'It isn't there any more,' she said, dully. She remembered the open fire, the pool table, the giant friendly dog that seemed to live on half-pints of bitter and prawn cocktail crisps. Had the two of them gone there a lot in their late teens? With Si and their other friends? She couldn't remember.

'You know the music shop I'm taking about though, right?'

She nodded.

'Well, this woman had come in wanting a guitar, and he'd spent all afternoon trying to sell her one and hadn't realised that she wasn't interested in guitars at all. She was just trying to get his number. She had

33

to spell it out to him in the end. You know what he was like.'

'What do you mean?'

'He wasn't a player. Whatever the word is. You know what I'm talking about. Wouldn't understand subtle flirting. The way he told it, she really had to throw herself at him before he understood what she was after.'

He was overegging this, but she was unresponsive.

'Right. And he started seeing her?'

He couldn't decide if the expression on her face was one of shock or disbelief. Si wasn't bad-looking. Not at all. He suddenly felt like defending the guy, which was ridiculous.

'He said he was. He had a picture of her on his phone. Showed me. A bit younger than him. Black and red hair. Glasses. If I'd have known you were so interested . . .'

She frowned at this. 'He was your friend,' she said. The emphasis on *your*. 'I'm just asking. Let's not talk about it any more.'

'Fine,' he said.

She was right though. Of the two of them, he was always a bit closer to Si than she was. They were at the age – taking their A Levels, preparing to go to university – when they'd all go out together in a gang, but other than the couples, the group would tend to split apart into the boys and the girls, like fourteen-year-olds at a school disco. He was probably, for a while, Si's best friend. Did teenage boys – young men, they were, really – have best friends? Had they been competing with each other all along, and he just hadn't noticed it?

'It can't have lasted,' she went on. 'I didn't see a girlfriend there. She'd have sat up at the front, wouldn't she?'

'It was just his mum and Mark on the front row,' he said.

She picked her phone up from the table, using her thumbprint to open it up. One of her best friends used to check her boyfriend's phone every night – he slept so deeply she could get his thumb onto the touchscreen and open it up without waking him. The boyfriend would have been better with a password, she thought, though her friend found nothing more sinister than a bit of Redtube in his internet history. She scrolled and scrolled, looking through Si's photographs, stopping on the ones where he was with someone else, with a woman.

'I don't see anything. What was she called?'

'Jessie. Jemima. Something like that. I don't re-member. Why?' He wished he hadn't started this now. Needed to keep track of the name he'd pulled out of thin air – *Jessie* – in case she brought this up again later.

'I might send her a card,' she said, without looking up.

This sounded improbable, and he was about to push her further when someone came into the booth – a big man wearing jeans and a rugby shirt. He was followed by his friend who was slightly smaller, with longish dark hair and a red shirt.

If he was honest with himself, he probably wouldn't have pursued the conversation even if the men hadn't sat right near them, involved them in their conversation, introduced themselves a couple of times (they were both very drunk – red-faced and sweating slightly, damp patches under the arms of their shirts, even though it was cold outside) and insisted, after a few minutes, in buying both of them drinks.

'No, really. It's fine. We were about to leave, actually,' she said. She sounded more like a Londoner then – not only the accent she'd acquired, but the way she spoke – a kind of clipped, disinterested confidence. Happier on her own, thanks.

'Oh come on,' the man in the red shirt said. 'We're strangers here. Just killing time. We're going to make our way over to Liverpool tomorrow.' He had an Irish accent. 'Or the day after. Then fly to Spain.' He turned to his friend. 'Whereabouts in Spain are we going?'

The man in the rugby shirt grinned delightedly. 'Not a clue. We'll decide when we get to the airport. See what we feel like.'

They were giddy, the two of them. Not just with drink. Giddy with news. Bursting to be asked.

'You on the run?' he said, then regretted it. He hadn't meant anything by it at all – he was just trying to fill in the gaps in the conversation that she, still swiping at her phone on the hunt for Si's imaginary girlfriend, was ostentatiously ignoring. But they were Irish, these guys. He didn't want them thinking he was implying they were terrorists, or something. He didn't think that. Hadn't even crossed his mind. Didn't want them to think that's what he thought. That he was that sort of idiot. How to correct this?

He closed his eyes and inhaled. Felt the heat on the sides of his neck. She could help him out here. She could say something. Change the subject or ask them a question about fucking Spain. It wouldn't kill her to be sociable. He exhaled slowly. He was just a bit drunk, that's all.

'We're on our travels,' red shirt clapped rugby shirt on the back so hard he nearly choked. 'Been all over the place. All over. We were in Edinburgh yesterday. Weren't we? Tell them where else we've been.'

Rugby shirt obliged, and while he spoke, drinks were obtained, brought to the table, finally accepted. Three pints of some kind of dark real ale that was bound to make him sick on top of the lager already fizzing about inside him, and something pink and yellow in a tall glass. Drink for the lady. She was ignoring it. They didn't seem to notice. Didn't seem to be offended. They were too happy: smirking like lunatics.

'We've won the lottery,' rugby shirt said. He was glowing. He smiled, showing all his teeth, jiggled in his seat, then laughed. Red shirt joined in, and they shook each other by the shoulders and knocked their foreheads together like brothers on Christmas morning. 'The fucking Euromillions!'

She watched them, distracted from her search for a moment. There was something infectious about this: about the utter drunken joy the pair of them were broadcasting all over the bar. She didn't know why she was so bothered about Simon's love life. Jemima or Jessie, or whatever her name was, was probably nothing more than a one-night stand, or even perhaps a bit of wishful thinking invented and embellished to impress the big man up on a visit from London.

'The pair of you?' she asked.

'We always share a ticket,' red shirt said, 'every week without fail. And never won a fucking note. Not once.'

'But last Friday, just gone,' rugby shirt said, 'we won the fucking jackpot. Between us!' He couldn't contain it. They stamped their feet, a little drum roll. The table they were all sitting at vibrated and froth slopped down the sides of the pint glasses.

She picked up her stupid drink, mainly to save it from the mucking about. It tasted like peaches. Not terrible, but, well. The lottery. They weren't saying exactly how much. *A life-changing amount, split down the middle*. That's the phrase he used.

'You lucky bastards,' he said, egging them on.

He asked them how they knew each other, and what they did when they realised they'd got the winning ticket, and what they were going to do with the money. It wasn't often she saw him like this – out of himself. He was always very drunk when he did the

Peter Kay impression. Now, he was merely tipsy, and carrying on with them like they were old friends.

She'd heard enough of this and went back to her phone, decided that no, Si hadn't had a girlfriend. There was nothing on his Facebook. He wasn't a heavy user and she'd been able to scroll back years. There was hardly anything there.

She looked at the last set of messages they'd sent each other – a year ago – and wondered if someone else had access to his account now – Mark, perhaps, using it to find his friends and contacts, or his mother, staying up late and downloading grainy mobile phone photographs taken in nightclubs from his online albums and printing them out. She should have considered that earlier.

Before she could think too much about digital footprints and memorials and lasting online legacies, she deleted the messages. Whether that meant they were gone from her inbox but would still exist in his, she didn't know.

When she looked up, the lottery winners – her drunk boyfriend's new best mates – were standing to leave. They were determined, they said, to do as they'd done in Edinburgh, and take a celebratory drink or two in every bar in the town before moving on. He was retelling them that old myth about Preston – more pubs per head than any other city in the country. More suicides too. She was sick of hearing it. The Peter Kay impression was only one more drink away. But the door lurched closed and the men left behind them a kind of muted, shell-shocked silence. She felt the rest of the pub sighing in relief.

'Well,' he said, pointlessly. He looked pleased.

'Do you think they'll make it to Liverpool tomorrow? They were in a bit of a state,' she said, pushing the ridiculous drink – half-empty now – away from her.

'They'll book a hotel room tonight. Like us.'

'To share?' she raised an eyebrow.

'No. They're not a couple. They work together. That's how they know each other.'

'You were getting on like a house on fire.'

'They were all right,' he said, and felt like she was accusing him of something. She was in a strange mood. Still clutching her phone. He decided to distract her. 'But let's say they did end up sharing. Say the hotel – the Travelodge, is it? – only has one room left, so they can have that or nothing. Last-minute booking. They think it's a twin, but it's a double.'

They used to do this together a lot, when they

first moved to London, sitting late at night on nearly empty carriages with their ears ringing with nightclub noise, making up things about the people – always strangers – they had met during their drinking hours.

'It's the Premier Inn,' she said.

'I stand corrected,' he mock-saluted her.

She smiled – she'd remembered their game now, he hoped – and yes, she joined in.

'They take the room. They don't think it's ideal – don't want people thinking they're a couple or anything. But they're also pissed, and it isn't as if they know anyone here they can crash with. And anyway, tomorrow, if they get up early enough, they can book twenty rooms in the best hotel in Liverpool, if they feel like it. Fly out from John Lennon to Madrid first-class, if they fancy. It's only one night.'

'Exactly. They're going to make the best out of it. Have a shower. A cup of tea in the room,' he tried to put on an Irish accent there, but it was terrible, and he saw her eyes flick away from him to the bar, to see if anyone else had heard. She was checking, even now, when things were OK and they were having fun. He corrected himself: *trying* to have fun. He was trying his fucking best to have a bit of fun with her, and she was checking the bar to see if anyone had noticed – if there was anyone worth feeling embarrassed in front of. He stopped.

'And he gets a bit fruity? A hand under the covers?' She giggled. It was just like her to bring it around to sex.

'No,' he shook his head. 'Nothing like that. The big guy – he falls asleep. Spark out. Flat on his back, on the bed with his clothes on. He's probably not been sober for a week. He starts snoring like a chainsaw.'

And they were back in.

'The other one – the dark-haired one – sits there on the end of the bed flicking through the channels for a while,' she added. 'He's just trying to find something to watch. There's nothing. Some film about a sick woman – *Steel Magnolias* – which he's not interested in. BBC Parliament. Nobody watches that. Not even pissed.'

She paused, and he took up the thread.

'He scrolls past BabeStation, which, as a feminist, he is offended by.' She laughed at this, and he was pleased – he still enjoyed making her laugh, even after everything. 'He turns the telly off. Just sits there, listening to his mate snoring. He knows he's not going to be able to sleep. Which gives him time to think. And after a while, he thinks about that ticket. About how he went to the shop and bought it. He was the one who chose the numbers.'

She nodded eagerly. 'Oh yes. And he does his sums. Works out that half of *a life-changing amount* is a lot – fair enough. He can buy the house he's renting, and a couple of cars, and pay off his mother's mortgage, and he can probably do some travelling, if there's anywhere else he feels like going.'

'He sits there for a bit, not noticing what's on the telly. And he draws his conclusions,' he said. 'The money – or rather – his half of it – isn't going to keep him for life. He'll have to invest it. Use his head and not get carried away. Buy a business. And what does he know about business, or investing? Why shouldn't he get carried away and spend it like it's water? But on only half, if he does that, in ten years' time – maybe less than that – he'll be back where he started.'

He paused, but she didn't pick up the story. She was sitting with her hand against her chest, fiddling with the neckline of her dress. It was a gesture she made when she was happy.

He carried on. 'So, our man looks at his friend, who is lying there, so fast asleep that nothing's going to wake him. They've both had a skinful, but he's always been able to hold his booze better, and he thinks of all that money – whether it will be a cheque or a bank transfer, and how in a few years he'll have nothing but a tall story to tell about it.'

'Yes. And they'll end up back home, where they started. Big men back from their travels, with everyone there just as they left them, laughing at them,' she said.

He shook his head. 'No. It won't be like that. No one will be there. They'll expect that. The big homecoming. Red carpet. Barman remembering their usual at the local. But things will have moved on. Children grown up. Old people died. Friends moved away. They'll get back with nothing much to show for themselves and there won't even be anyone there to tell a tall story to. It won't be home any more. And he thinks about all of that and how different it would be if he had the entire amount to himself. Enough, maybe, to fake his own death and disappear from home completely.'

She was intent on him. Wanting to know the end to this story.

'And so, before he knows it, there's a pillow in his hands, and the entire time he's holding it, his friend's legs kicking around on the bed, he's thinking only two things – one, that people who get very very very drunk can just die in their sleep, suffocating on their own tongues and it's a tragedy, but a self-inflicted one. And two...'

She burst out laughing, which was good, because he didn't know what the second thing should be. Something about his mother, perhaps. Or travel. He didn't know. You can ruin a story by looking too hard for a punchline, can't you?

'It sounds like a Patricia Highsmith novel,' she said.

He tilted his head in mock modesty.

'What would you want to buy, if we won the lottery?' she asked.

'We don't buy tickets. We've never bought a ticket. Have we?'

'We haven't! Should we? Should we start buying tickets? Or scratch cards? I'm thirty-seven years old and I've never even bought a scratch card.'

'And after the way you misspent your youth, too,' he said. 'I'm surprised at you.'

They were at their best when they were like this. The teasing. The double act, put on to entertain nobody but themselves. Which was why it surprised him – the way being woken from a comfortable sleep by a punch to the back of the head feels surprising

— when she lined up her glass on the beer mat carefully, bit her bottom lip and looked right at him while she said:

'IVF. That's what I'd buy. It's six thousand pounds a go, and most couples with unexplained fertility need three cycles. More, if you're over thirty-five.'

She waited. He said nothing. She was determined to wait him out, to say nothing else until he answered her – or at least acknowledged what she'd said properly, but another thought came and she couldn't help herself.

'Even private places have waiting lists. I suppose if you have enough money you could skip the queue. *A life-changing amount.*'

She waited. Only a second or two passed until he did what he always does at moments like this, which was to awkwardly pat her arm – as if she'd just told him that an unpleasant and distant relative had died and the funeral was inconveniently timed – then look away – at something interesting he'd found to stare at over her head.

But she knew it didn't matter. Because in those two seconds before his hand came out to touch her arm, she had so carefully stage-managed his ideal reaction to what she'd just said – which yes, of course, was below the belt and manipulative and the wrong time, but when would there be a right time, when would he ever sit down and say, 'so, how do you feel about the fact that we've been trying, on and off, for about eighteen months now, and nothing's happened, and should we talk about that, do you think?' – that whatever he did next was bound to fall short. Her ideal, imaginary boyfriend – an improbably better man – would have gathered her in his arms, or presented, inexplicably, flowers, or some other subservient gesture of relief and adoration that they both knew he just did not feel any more. She bit her bottom lip again. Refused to say anything else. *Your turn.*

'That much,' he said eventually, as if she'd just told him how much a new dress cost. Any minute now, he would claim he needed to go to the toilet. That was the point where she should have changed the subject (the mood between them had cooled rapidly, of course), but she was persistent.

'I don't know. It was ages ago that I looked it up. It's more if you use a donor.'

'You've looked that up? Donors?'

She watched him turn away from her, lower his head and start flipping the beer mat off the edge of the table. He caught it before it fell, lined it up, and flicked it again.

'Eggs. People donate eggs too. I wasn't . . .'

She can't talk to him about anything without him acting like she's about to beat him up. It didn't matter what approach she tried. Too gentle and subtle, and he ignored it. Too obvious, and he acted like she'd slapped him. It was pointless. She sighed heavily and finished her stupid drink. The sugar caught the back of her throat and she felt sick and thirsty and pissed off, all at the same time. There was a long pause, during which he took his cigarette packet out of his pocket, opened it, inspected his supply, then replaced it.

He imagined what they looked like, the pair of them sitting here together, as cold and as awkward as the couple from that Hemingway story.

'I was going to say I'd buy a ticket on one of those space shuttle things. Richard Branson is building one. You can go into orbit. Only millionaires will ever be able to afford it, but winning the lottery is a bit more likely than me becoming an astronaut.'

'Space?'

'Yes,' he nodded.

'You'd spend millions of pounds on going into

space? Not to land on the moon or Mars or anything. But just going up there, having a look, and coming back again?'

'It's not millions of pounds. Half a million. Something like that. But yes, if we won the lottery, I definitely would,' he said, 'in a heartbeat.'

She laughed – not quite bitterly, but getting there. She laughed because she was imagining him strapped into a shiny tin can, like something from a 1950s space travel comic – a little boy's dream. Looking out through a porthole into the blackness of infinite space, feeling immense relief, no doubt, at the extent of his solitude.

'Virgin Orbit. Virgin Galactic. Something like that.'

'It sounds like porn,' she said. 'One of the channels after BabeStation.'

'Virgin Orbit. Naughty Girls in Space,' he put on his American news presenter voice, and she looked away and did not laugh. 'Do you remember what Si used to say about the fireworks?'

He knew full well he was only trying to distract her – of course he did. But he also really had just remembered sitting on a wall somewhere with Si after they'd been to a nightclub. In the memory they are both eating chips with garlic and chilli mayonnaise – almost as much mayonnaise as chips – from polystyrene clamshells. It wasn't a wall they were sitting on; it was the steps outside St John's Minster, at the back end of town.

He could see it now: the big dark church behind them, with its clock face and grey steeple. The takeaway opposite. A queue for the taxi rank snaking along the wet pavement. That was it. They would have been finishing their chips while they waited for the queue to go down. In no rush to get home. And he had been depressed, Si. That's what the night out had been about – cheering him up. Everyone else was going off to university and Si was waiting behind, and they were worried about him, in the kind of self-absorbed, magnanimous way of teenagers. Had he said he was depressed? Or had the rest of them just assumed that? He'd had more money than any of them, and bought a round of drinks for everyone – an adult gesture unheard of.

'He said that when he died he wanted to get cremated and we should put his ashes inside a firework and shoot it off into the sky,' he said. Out loud, it sounded silly – the kind of thing a lonely, slightly drunk and morbid seventeen-year-old would say. Not the kind of thing any adult would do.

'You'll have to let his mother know. I'm sure she'd appreciate that,' she laughed cruelly. 'I can just imagine her telling the undertaker's. Why don't you phone her up?'

He took her laugh for genuine amusement and was smiling, relaxed, thinking the storm – and the threat of it – was over now. He had been able to charm her away from the danger zone for tonight.

He gulped the last two inches of his pint, stood, and lifted his empty glass and hers, still thinking of Si – the way his jeans were always too long for him and were frayed at the back where his heels caught on them as he walked. He only seemed to have three T-shirts – a ZERO one, with the star, a Che Guevara one, and a New Model Army one. He wondered what he wore today. Inside that box. His mum will have found a suit for him. People get cremated in suits. Off to the little fire in their Sunday best. He wanted to laugh at this, though he didn't know why. He waggled the glasses at her.

'I'm going to take these back. Shall we have another, or do you want to go?'

He was looking relaxed and playful in a way she

hadn't seen him look for months. Longer than that. A year, she supposed. It wasn't only the booze – she'd seen him drunk plenty of times, and usually it sent him into a funk, more morose and monosyllabic than usual. Perhaps it was the thought of space. Isn't that what he was always asking for?

She could let this go – it would be very easy to – but in a tiny act of sadism, she said, 'I'm not assuming we'd need a donor. They'd test us first. Both of us. But if it came down to it, I'd take an egg. If they said that was what it would take. I'd do that.'

He flinched. Standing there, his fingers inside the two glasses, holding them together. There was nobody sitting near them now, but he whispered anyway.

'We don't need donations of anything. We did . . . It happened. Before.'

This was his own act of sadism. She would certainly abandon this subject for the evening now he'd said that. She closed her eyes for a second, then pulled her jacket on and stood up.

'We can go somewhere else. I'll pick this time, though.'

'OK,' he said. 'OK. You're in charge.'

THE OLDE DOG AND PARTRIDGE, FRIARGATE

SHE LOOKED AROUND the pub as she waited. It wasn't comfortable, sitting on the low stool at the round table. Almost everyone else was standing, which meant her view, apart from the clear space around the pool table, comprised of the denim- and leather-clad crotches of the people standing around her. The air was wet, heavy. It smelled like cigarettes, weed and old ashtrays, even though everyone who smoked lined up outside to do it, carrying on conversations by text, or through the open windows.

'Do you need both of those stools, love?' a man with a beard – not the hipster kind, but a proper one – leaned down and shouted at her. She shook her head and smiled at him and he carried one of the spare stools away.

The music was loud and in front of the bar a few women were half-heartedly dancing, moving from foot to foot while carrying on a conversation with an extremely tall man – he must be six feet five, at least, she thought – wearing a leather jacket with bleached yellow hair plaited down his back. A Viking. He wasn't dancing, just standing there like their maypole.

I'm pissed, she thought. A little overdressed too. She looked down at herself, took off the black cardigan and twitched the top of the dress downwards a little. Better? There was nobody to ask.

Why had she brought him here? Force of habit? Revenge? They used to come here all the time. Underage. They all did. Perhaps things were a bit tighter these days. She looked around again and didn't see any teenagers. Instead she was surrounded by the adults they must have grown into, most of them the same age or older than her, and, she realised, the friends she made then were not friends for life at all, because where were they today? Where are they now?

There were some trestle tables and benches under an arch towards the back end of the pub, a little lower down, and that's where they all used to sit, making a couple of pints last all night, playing cards, and pooling coins for the jukebox. She looked over there for the ghosts of her old friends – and for herself, before all of this, but instead she saw a group of men sitting there, playing some elaborate game with coloured cards and dice with too many sides. She stared for a while and caught nobody's eye.

Where was he, with the drinks?

She put the cardigan back on. She had only chosen this place because, last year, after a cancelled connection between London and a conference in Glasgow and an urgent desire to avoid having to spend the night in her father's spare room, she came here for a drink with Si, who happened to be the first one to respond to a text she'd sent to all the friends whose numbers she still had.

It had been awkward, and he'd made a remark about their hometown not being northern at all but right at the centre of the island they lived on. He'd shared the fact proudly – as if he really did feel like he lived at the centre of the earth – that to be here was a gift of some kind. He'd always been like that: blessed with a capacity for happiness – with the conviction (she might not have phrased it like that at the time – had mainly found him irritating) that he was extremely lucky. He spoke about gratitude a lot.

Three drinks in, she had – in a way that had offended him slightly – said that the short distance to both London and Glasgow and the ease of getting to either was the best thing about home, and when was he going to get out, like the rest of them had? He'd smiled patiently and had not allowed himself to be riled. So she'd persisted. It wasn't like he was stupid, she'd said. It wasn't like he didn't have anything going for him. Only a lack of direction.

Even thinking about this conversation now had the capacity to make her cringe: the way her voice had been too loud, broadcasting her unwanted advice across the bar.

Then they'd got onto Brexit – this was the month after the referendum – and the post-industrial North whose populations were too under-informed to really understand what they'd been voting for. It had been unnecessary and cruel and arrogant – she knew it even at the time – and what's worse is that after four or five drinks she'd ended up sleeping with him.

On the table in front of her there was a yellow flier for a band who would be playing at a pub around the corner the following week. She folded it up into a tiny rectangle, unfolded it, then started to refold it along its creases. Bringing him here would have been tantamount to rubbing his face in it, she supposed. A kind of revenge for that business about going into space. Except he didn't have a clue, and they were hardly likely to run into Si now.

She had not been able to develop the necessary excuse she needed to square what she had done with the image she'd like to have of herself. The effort to achieve this was exhausting and yet she persisted in it. It was during a period when she'd become homesick: very homesick. Sick of London too, of the Inspector Sands announcements in the tube stations and the relentless trudge back and forth to work, standing crammed onto the tube, reading proofs of books she couldn't convince anyone to buy while leaning against strangers. The way her clothes smelled all the time: sweat and cigarette smoke and exhaust fumes and fried food. The expense of everything – the rent and the Oyster cards – and every night, another trip on the tube to some bookshop or gallery or events space, to drink warm wine from plastic cups and oversee a fumbled reading, lacklustre Q and A and the selling of a mere handful of paperbacks. All that was true.

And in the midst of this, and her obnoxious ranting, Si had taken her hand and pulled her out into the night and they'd walked through the town and he had been so kind to her. They were going to go to his car, he'd said, and he was going to take her to his flat, pick up his bike, and they were going out for a spin.

'Are you too pissed to hold on tight?' he'd asked. And she'd shaken her head. 'I've got a spare helmet. Come on. Let's get the wind in your hair. Three times round the ring road, full throttle, and you'll be a new woman.'

'My shoes,' she'd said, gesturing towards her kitten heels and feeling disgusted with herself as soon as the words were out of her mouth. 'Shit. I can't believe I've just said that. Fuck my shoes.'

'You need to give yourself a break,' he'd said. 'Talk a bit less. Think a bit less, if you can manage it,' and then he'd kissed her – not that kind of kiss – as they'd waited to cross the road towards the car park.

She'd turned his peck on her cheek into something else.

'What's this?' he'd said. And he didn't look surprised. That was the thing that had really pissed her off. She'd expected shock, or even gratitude. Hadn't he always had a bit of a thing for her? Instead, there was a mild kind of warmth on his part. He was not unwilling, was the general gist, but she was going to have to spell it out for him.

'What do you think it is?' she'd said, and kissed him again.

Maybe she'd been trying to make some kind of apology for her behaviour. Maybe just get out of the bike ride.

And him? Maybe he really was lonely, left behind here all on his own. Maybe it was revenge, not against her, but against her boyfriend, who hadn't visited often enough. Something like that.

They'd gone and done it in his car, no less. It had been a fumbling, unpleasant sort of thing. Her boyfriend had been back in Lewisham, working, not invited to the conference she was on her way back from.

None of these things were reasons, not really. Just the landscape her decision had taken place in. A general wanting to go home, without quite being able to admit it. A wish to return, to have everything move backwards. She'd told nobody, but imagined telling a friend, and that friend diagnosing her with a mid-life crisis, which all the millennials got at age thirty because they were precocious and self-indulgent about this, as well as everything else. It was par for the course. A *bit grim* (that's the word her friend would use to mean something unpleasant but harmless) but best forgotten about. It was too shameful to talk about. And anyway, she was a bit too old to be a millennial, wasn't she?

Nothing had come of it. It wasn't like she'd had an affair. And Si was his friend, yes, but not exactly his best friend, not really. She'd not quite kept in touch, but not taken steps to prevent him from contacting her either. It was easy enough to stay away from her hometown: that might have been one of the reasons she'd done it – to burn a bridge once and for all.

Time had passed and she'd considered the offence buried. She does understand how paltry her reasons were: being drunk, feeling old and unmoored, wanting to be at home somewhere. She does know that.

She looked around for him again. What she should do was stand up and find him and tell him she'd changed her mind about this pub. Too busy. Too many ghosts. Not their scene any more. She should find him and take his arm and get him back out onto Friargate. There were nightclubs and restaurants and nicer bars further along. Or just the hotel. There was no need to cause him unnecessary hurt (that's what her imaginary confidante would have advised).

Though every time the two of them argued – quite a lot, these days – she'd considered throwing the news at him like a bomb and ending the disagreement by blowing the entire house down. The thought of it gives her vertigo sometimes. The power. All this (which is the flat, with the flimsy front door, the tiny round table squashed into the living room, a place to cook that was not a kitchen but a kitchenette, a bedroom too small for a proper wardrobe, the MacBooks and shared Netflix account and direct debits and the little bowl on the coffee table they keep the wallets and keys and Starbucks loyalty cards in) only stands and continues because she has kept this nasty little thing to herself. She kept their entire lives running by keeping quiet. Sometimes she thinks he would be a bit grateful to her for her silence, if only he knew about it.

And it really was nothing. A ten-minute shag. If that. It would have been nothing. A nasty thing. A lapse, best forgotten. Except, five weeks after she'd come home from that last trip to Preston, he'd caught her vomiting the half-cup of coffee she'd just drunk into the bathroom sink. Their eyes met in the mirror as she wiped her mouth.

'I'm not hungover,' she'd said. 'It must be a bug.'

'Are you sure?' he'd asked. He raised his eyebrows, suddenly – nobody surprised at this more than him – excited.

*

He waited near the bar. It was busy, but he could have been served earlier. He kept nudging himself backwards. Letting other people drift in front of him. It had been ten minutes. A woman with purple and black eye make-up on and spiky blue-black hair noticed him.

'You were here before me, love. Go on,' she gestured towards the bar.

'It's all right,' he said, 'you go. I haven't decided what I want yet.'

He stepped back, pretending to study the blackboards behind the bar where the guest ales were listed in chalk. He used to know the people who worked here, but he doesn't any more. Of course not. It meant it was a bit easier to avoid catching their eyes.

Another two minutes passed. How could the noise in here be so loud – people shouting at each other – and still, he wasn't able to make out a single word of all the conversations bubbling on around him? He was either giving her time to settle down, or avoiding her. He allowed himself to believe that it was the first – that he was just allowing her a moment of space – but he knew he was letting himself off the hook.

He was still thinking of Si and his fireworks. Half

the guys in this pub looked like him. At their last meeting, after Lila's christening earlier that year, Si had wanted to hug him, to shake his hand, and he'd refused both – only patting his former friend on the arm as they'd parted ways outside the pub. There'd been an awkward pause then, as the goodbyes had been said but they were both still there, searching for cigarettes and looking up and down the street, wondering about taxis.

'Let's just leave it there,' he'd said, as if this was a meeting at work, no agreement reached, and the consensus to table the decision until next month. 'It was a bit ago now. No point in . . .' He'd never finished his sentence. It was inadequate. He had been, he realised, inadequate to the situation. Simon had been expecting something he had been unable to provide. A fight in the street? A tearful embrace?

Now he stood, still dithering at the bar, and was unable to order because he kept seeing the familiar outline of his friend out of the corner of his eye, and in the space where feeling should be, there was nothing.

Where was he with her wine? There was still no sign. He'd either met someone he knew or had decided to step outside to smoke before going to the bar. She felt like an idiot, sitting there at a table on her own without a drink. His jacket was on his empty stool, and she lifted it – to stop it sliding onto the floor, she told herself, but as soon as it was in her hand she felt the weight of his phone in his inside pocket, and, looking towards the window (the word *furtive* came to mind – unjustly, she thought), she took the phone out of his pocket and folded the jacket over her knee and pressed her thumb against the lock screen. When the phone rejected her print and asked her for a passcode instead, she put in her own birthday, then the date they met, then his birthday, then their home phone number, minus the area code, and finally she was in.

The messages showed nothing of interest. Practical, 'bring back some milk, would you?' type exchanges between the two of them, or arrangements to meet between him and a couple of friends. He wasn't a texter. His last five emails were from eBay, YouTube and Spotify. His photos were practical too: pictures of instruction manuals, of the back of their wireless router – the part that shows the password – or of the hinges on their front gate, which he kept saying he was going to ask their landlord to replace. There was a photograph of her in there too. In the picture she is lying in their bed – a Sunday morning a few months ago, it must have been – awake, but her eyes closed against the thin sunlight, which streamed into the room when he jumped up and opened the curtains, and suggested they go out for a bike ride. She'd lain there like that, half hoping he'd take the photo, or get back into bed with her. And he had.

She closed the photo app. What was she looking for? She doesn't suspect him of having an affair. She'd almost be pleased if it turned out he was fucking – or at least trying to fuck, in his self-effacing, slightly awkward way – one of the girls from work. There were plenty to choose from. Stick-thin twenty-year-olds with pastel trousers and brogues and big jewellery. He'd be terrified of a girl like that, of course, but even the thought of him attempting it would make her feel better.

She returned to the emails, but there was nothing but a couple of confirmations from Virgin Trains. She scrolled past their subject lines with a growing sense of frustration.

He could at least be sexting someone. She'd be relieved at that. The secrecy a hidden relationship would involve would generate in him an interior world that she had never been able to find, nor see evidence of otherwise. She'd be less lonely in her guilt if she knew he was having an affair: if she knew he was the kind of person that had messy, human desires, and disreputable secrets, and who made a balls-up of things now and again.

He had the SoundCloud app, and she opened it, wondering what kind of music he was listening to these days. There was just one file there. She pressed play. The file lasted twenty-three seconds and it was called 'beat' and she heard nothing, so set it to play again, pressing the phone's speaker against her ear. The clamour in the pub diminished as she withdrew her attention from it, and there – she could just about make out an underwater whooshing sound, the sound she heard in the flat when she was lying submerged in the bath and he put the washing machine on. A patter on top of that. A fast, regular patter. There was a ripple to this sound: a kind of echo. Behind the echo, the rushing sound of water. One more play, and she got it, and was stunned.

Your turn, the phone seemed to say.

She'd been embarrassed when he'd asked the sonographer to turn up the volume on the machine as loud as it would go, then pointed his phone at it. She'd been lying there, top up, trousers down, her still-flat belly lubed up and goosepimpled with cold.

And he'd been inches from the screen, recording everything. She'd been irritated at the time. He looked like one of those awful people who whipped out their phone at the scene of an accident. Someone who held a tablet overhead at a concert and ruined the view for everyone else. She'd never asked him to replay what he'd captured. But he still had it.

She felt a great rush of tenderness, and looked around for him, wanting to hug him tightly. To comfort him in the pain he didn't know he suffered. She stopped. She quickly closed SoundCloud, then locked the phone. Slipped it back into his suit pocket, then folded the jacket and held it against herself. When he came back, he found her like this, hunched over and holding his suit jacket against her like a child.

'Are you cold?' he asked, and she shook her head.

'Just pissed.'

He laughed at this.

'You won't want these then?'

He had a pint for himself and an enormous glass of wine for her – one of those glasses that holds a third of a bottle. And chasers too.

'You trying to take advantage of me?' she said. She'd meant to flirt, but it came out sounding crabby and suspicious.

'We should drink to him,' he said, nodding at the whisky. He swilled it around in his glass. 'If he's not getting fireworks, he should at least get a toast. Don't you think?'

She raised the little glass. They clinked together.

'To Si,' he said. He was watching her carefully.

She tried to smile, but she was tired and her face wasn't working properly. She drank the whisky and shuddered.

'I hate drinking spirits. You're supposed to have the whisky afterwards,' she said.

'Whisky before wine, you'll feel fine,' he said. 'Isn't that how it works?'

She covered her mouth with the back of her hand and burped slightly.

'Sorry. Cheers. I'm surprised you didn't say you'd buy a house,' she said. 'That's what I thought you'd say.'

He considered this. They'd been saving a long time.

'I don't think even a *life-changing amount* would get us somewhere liveable in Zone 2,' he said. He thought about their savings account. The house deposit money – a laughably small and un-life-changing figure for all their years of scrimping. 'We'd have to go into the suburbs. Home Counties.'

She laughed at this. 'Right. And you can give up your job and stay at home decorating cupcakes and walking the dog in your Hunter wellies. Popping to Waitrose twice a week in the Range Rover.'

They both shuddered theatrically.

'Not that then.'

'No.'

He looked at her as she sipped her wine. She was suffering, of course. He'd been watching her carefully for signs of grief, but it wasn't that – or at least, it didn't seem to be. She'd cried a little at the funeral. He counted two tears that she had caught at the corner of her eye and dabbed away with her index finger before they spoiled her make-up. Nothing more than that. She hadn't cried the night they'd got Mark's Facebook messages. Hadn't cried on the long train journey up. Hadn't cried at the wake. She wasn't, as far as he'd been able to tell, pining for him. Locked into her grief. It wasn't that.

He tried to feel guilty for lying to her. Simon hadn't mentioned anything about a girlfriend when he was up for Lila's christening. No Jessie. No Jemima. They'd had a pint, sure, but the story about the girl in the guitar shop he'd just made up, on the hoof. Partly to see what she'd do. To see if it would jag her – if she minded. He had called Si and there had been talk of a game of pool, but after the christening they'd met – not at this pub, but at a little one around the corner (The Brit, was it? He can't remember any more) and sat next to each other drinking pints. At first they told themselves they were waiting for the pool table to become free. Had even searched for the right coins in their change to slip onto the side and claimed their place in the queue. Simon had asked about the christening, about how old Lila was now. Was she walking? How old were babies when they learned to walk? Neither of them knew. He had bragged a little about his job and their flat in London. And eventually he began to get a picture of what Si wanted to tell him, and was finding so hard to spit out. The bragging – an attempt at connecting with his old friend through an old sense of competitiveness – had probably made it easier for Simon to stick the boot in.

'I just thought you should know,' he'd said.

But this wasn't an attempt to clear his conscience. There might have been an element of half-hearted revenge, perhaps – he was only human, after all. But it was mainly an attempt at connection.

'Look,' Simon was saying – or trying to – 'what a mess we've all made of things.'

He'd batted it back.

'Well you've told me now,' he'd said sourly. And nothing else.

The news had not been a surprise. He had suspected this – not since her night alone in Preston – no, not immediately – but definitely since he'd added up the dates around her pregnancy and watched her stony-faced and unmoved in the aftermath of her miscarriage. To be honest, he had been suspecting this for years. He was always – he recognised in that moment – faintly surprised whenever he heard her key in the lock and realised she had come home to him again.

'I'm so sorry you lost the baby,' he'd said, mechanically, on the day she laid on the couch staring at the television.

'We'll try again in a few weeks,' she'd said, without emotion, 'do it better this time. It'll be fine. It doesn't matter.'

That's how he'd known.

And he could have told Simon. Could have told him about the pregnancy, and the dates, and the miscarriage. Could have stuck the boot in himself.

But he hadn't. Had kept quietly to himself the thing that did matter – not because it was or wasn't his, but because it had been hers, and she hadn't been able to want this one.

'Shall we have one last drink?' he said.

They were in the middle of a conversation they'd had many times before about property prices and shared ownership and the outrageous state of the housing market in the capital. In a moment, they'd return to one of their favourite topics – how much they hate Baby Boomers – but then he lifted his empty glass and brandished it at her.

'Go on. For Si.'

'I don't know. Haven't we had enough? I feel sick.'

They were out of sync now: he'd probably suggest a nightclub in a minute. They were never going to be able to buy a house. Not unless they came home – here – where they could probably buy an entire flat on what they'd saved already. The place where they started from was looming large as their final destination whether they liked it or not. Maybe it wouldn't be so bad. Simon had had a flat. She wondered if it was his. If he'd just been renting it. She wondered about the things he'd left behind, and whose job it would be to sort them out. The girlfriend? Why hadn't they ever asked him? How had it been possible for them both to lose interest in him so entirely?

'Just one more. Come on. Or it's the hotel room, and we'll only get miserable.'

He held a hand out to her, and she took it, and he pulled her upwards gently. Their faces were quite close together for a moment – half a second, if that – and there wasn't time enough for her to wonder if he was going to kiss her, though of course he wouldn't, not in public (hardly in private, either), but he did, on her cheek, like she was a cousin, or someone else's girlfriend. Like she was only someone he used to know – someone he had been seeing for a while, ages and ages ago, and had no hard feelings for but could barely remember.

WETHERSPOON'S

THERE WAS NO horror like a town-centre Wetherspoon's on a Thursday night. He knew even as they crossed the road that there was no way they were going to get a seat. Despite the rain, which had turned the pavement a shiny tar-black, there was a crowd of smokers outside the front doors so numerous they had spilled down the steps on the approach and were gathering in the street.

On the corner, there was a giant billboard advertising opportunities at a town-centre FE college – the one they both went to. The photograph on the board was of a smiling young man wearing a welder's mask, giving a thumbs up to the camera. He squeezed her hand, about to point it out to her, but they were across the road now and he had to nudge and apologise his way through the vaping and smoking crowd to get up the stairs and into the pub.

It was no less crowded inside. Half of Preston must have been in there. Men in dark jeans, shined shoes and good shirts. Women in brightly coloured clothes, their hair straightened or curled or pinned up high or otherwise taken care of. He was still holding her hand, tugging her along behind him, and felt her turn her heel and topple slightly. She caught herself on the back of his jacket, and they carried on.

The queue at the bar was three deep, and the noise was something else – a many-layered river of sound, from the deep rumble of chatter, to the high notes of shrieked laughter and women calling to each other across the bar, or between tables, to the bubble of the music – something current and forgettable. There was a free table, though, tucked in next to a rack of mayonnaise and mustard and vinegar and tartar sauce packets, and baskets full of napkin-wrapped sets of cutlery.

'Over there,' he pointed towards it and she went and sat, spreading out his jacket and her bag across the other seats, then waited. The pattern on the carpet – geometric, purple and burgundy, printed with a pattern that was either entirely random or extremely regular – tumbling matchsticks? – compelled his gaze, then threatened to trip him as he made his way across it towards the bar. He looked away and found the design's after-image on his retina, floating on the pale-coloured walls.

It was massive in there. Felt like a sports hall – the atmosphere had that bright, harsh echo to it that school did: the glare in the corridors, the sense of exposure. Every now and again the sound of a dropped glass, or a raucous cheer. Banter. That was what he could hear. He was still, incredibly, on his way to the bar. It seemed to him that all the other drinking he had done this evening had been to prepare him for this, now, waving a folded twenty between his first two fingers and feeling a man crushed in so tight behind him he could tell the other man's shirt was damp.

When he got back to the table, she stood immediately and motioned towards the bathroom.

'Sorry,' she said, and he nodded her away. It wasn't like they could carry on a conversation here anyway. He wished, despite himself, for the cool silence he hoped would be waiting for him in the hotel room.

There was a newspaper on the table and he picked it up. The front-page headline made him smile: more local outrage about the pedestrianisation of the city centre and the inadequate parking arrangements.

Inside, letters of complaint about the 'eyesore' of the new addition to the train station (he hadn't noticed it himself), and endless rumbling debate about the fate of the bus station – listed building, brutalist masterpiece, admired by those who lived elsewhere and owned coffee-table photo books about it, despised by those who actually had to use it. She'd sneer at all of it. He almost checked the date on the newspaper, convinced that the headlines and the letters were precisely the same the last time he'd visited – feeling an absurd sense of pride, affection and nostalgia – when his guts lurched as he noticed the article about Simon.

Bike. Not heart. Not cancer. Not suicide. It was his bike. He read it quickly, the small newsprint dancing unsteadily before his eyes. He got the gist of it. Speeding through a junction outside of town, on one of his night rides. Wet roads, heavy weather, and – though the article didn't come out and say this – probably his own fault. He had been wearing a helmet-cam and that was how they could be so certain. It had recorded his speed and route, the view through his visor as he'd flown from his bike, somersaulted through the air and landed – not gracefully – on a verge by the side of the dual carriageway.

'Emma . . . ?' He looked up as he called for her,

certain that he'd just heard her voice. He wanted to show her the newspaper. But she wasn't there.

He drank more and reread the article. He must be more pissed than he realised because time was passing strangely now. He was still looking at the newspaper – the photograph of Si looking neater and happier than he ever did in real life – in front of him. But his drink was gone. The wine he'd bought for her gone too. And where was she?

He folded the paper and left it face down on the table, gathered their things and went to find her.

Would she have gone back to the hotel without him? It wasn't the best night they'd ever had, sure, but he couldn't say that they were on bad terms. Not really.

He waited outside the toilets for a while, counting women go in and out in pairs and threes. Their laughter bounced around his skull: he felt it vibrating through his jaw. His stomach rolled. He needed nothing more to drink and, leaning against the wall, tried to figure out what the framed pictures opposite were, but found they were nothing – watercolours of views from a moving car on a rainy day, perhaps – until he squinted and they resolved themselves into views of Avenham Park and the river in their Victorian heyday.

'You waiting for someone?' the woman had to repeat herself and finally he fixed on her face and nodded.

'Yes. She all right?'

She smiled warmly. 'You'd better go in, son. I think I heard someone being sick. Birthday, is it?'

He laughed knowingly. He wasn't sure why.

'We should have eaten before coming out,' he said, by way of explanation. 'We'll be rough as dogs in the morning.'

'Does you good now and again,' she said, and slipped away.

He went right in and called for her – more loudly than he needed to, because her name was his alibi. One of the cubicle doors opened slightly.

'In here. I'm all right.'

'Shall I bring you some water?'

'I'm in here,' she said again.

He edged into the cubicle and slid the lock closed behind him. It always leapt up at her like this – the drink – one minute she was sociable and a little flushed, the next she was argumentative, tearful, then barely conscious. He should have been looking out for the warning signs. Sometimes he could tell when she was blackout drunk and wouldn't remember a thing he said to her the next morning. Her eyes got blank and sharky. But now, sitting there on the pan, she just looked pale and clammy, her mascara slightly blurred.

'The state of you,' he said, with affection. 'Get up. I found a newspaper,' he grabbed her arm and lifted her up off the toilet. She put her hand on his shoulder and he leant in, helping her with her underwear. 'Were you sick? There was a woman outside said she heard someone being sick.'

'I'm not sick. Just tired. I just drifted off a little bit. It's been a long day. The travelling,' she waved an arm and let him tug at the hem of her dress, making her decent.

'You're drunk,' he said. He did want to kiss her now. It was against the law, wasn't it, to put the moves on your girlfriend when she was out of it? Fair enough. But seeing her like this – soft and guilty and needing him for something, for once – made him feel warm towards her. It wasn't sex. Not that. He just wanted to hold her. He kissed her head, but she shrugged him off.

'I'm not drunk,' she said, indignantly.

'There was a newspaper on the table,' he said, shouting at her a bit, as if she was deaf. He wanted her to hear him, but not to remember. She probably wouldn't remember. He kissed her head again. 'There was a bit in it about Simon. It was his bike. He didn't do it himself. It was his bike. He came off his bike.'

She stared at him. He took her arm and guided her out of the cubicle, meeting a woman on her way in. He was about to explain, but she smiled at him ruefully – the 'we've all been there' face of the heavy drinker. He smiled back, suddenly feeling very light.

'He came off his bike?' She started crying. 'That's so sad. It's really sad. Isn't it? He was young. Only our age. We should have stayed in touch with him.'

'It's all right,' he said. He couldn't give her a tissue or wipe her face because he was holding her up, so he just let her cry and gently kept her moving, pulling her past the sinks and hand dryers. They weren't real tears. She was only drunk. The place was all mirrors. Someone had drawn a smiley face in the corner of one of them in brown lipstick, and he tried to look at that instead of the pair of them, crumpled in their funeral clothes, worse for wear, slightly past their best, and – the realisation was sudden, albeit arguably rather belated – at the end of their drinking hours. Home time.

'He was our friend,' she said again, in the unmistakable tones of the self-pitying drunk, 'we never visited him.'

'Is that why you wouldn't let us come back at Christmas?' he said, already knowing the answer. 'Why we're not allowed to even *talk* about moving back home?'

'It isn't home,' she said forcefully.

'He didn't do himself in because he was pining for you,' he said quietly. 'So you can be relieved about that.'

She didn't respond. Probably hadn't even heard him. He carried on speaking quietly, not quite under his breath. He did this sometimes, when she was asleep. Getting it all off his chest while she gently snored, blissfully unaware of his rage.

'I didn't tell him about the baby. The miscarriage. Whatever we're calling it. He didn't do himself in because of that, either.'

She was still sniffing, looking around her, at the lights, the people pushing past and angling themselves to squeeze through towards the bar and the toilets.

'*Whatever we're calling it?*'

'I didn't mean it like that.'

'The fuck you did,' she said, nonsensically. He wanted to laugh.

'He never knew about that. I know about it. He never knew about it.'

83

It had become impossible for him to convey with any precision what he wanted to tell her. He'd lost his grip on it already. Could only think of Simon and that bike, that final spinning through the air like a Catherine wheel unmoored from the pole it had been fastened on to.

'I can't bear all of this,' she said, covering her face. 'I just want it all to stop. Can't you stop it? Wheedling at me?'

'You're not in some Channel 5 film, darling,' he muttered, his face turned away from her. He should have been feeling great relief, but instead he only knew that he sounded ridiculous. He had planned saying something like this to her for months. A statement that would cut her entirely down to size and show her that not only her offence, but she herself was nothing, beneath notice, hardly worth thinking about. But in his fantasies he managed to do it without sounding like a total tool, as he was now.

They were still moving through the crowd, slowly. Sometimes he had her hand in his, sometimes it slipped, and he was forced to tug at her wrist.

'This is real life,' he said, finally.

That didn't sound much better. A man standing near him turned – too suddenly – so that liquid spilled from his glass onto his shirt and he let go of her for a moment to show the man the palms of his hands, to be conciliatory, to accept his apology whole-heartedly. The last thing either of them needed now was a fist fight over a spilled pint of cider. Though he did feel like hitting something. Himself?

He reached back and found her wrist again. Tugged her closer and wrapped his arm around her shoulders.

'You didn't stay in touch with him,' she said, trying to pull away from him.

She was suddenly petulant and stubborn, as she could be when she was drunk, but he held tight, fearing that she would fall if he let go of her. Her funeral shoes had only small heels, but still she was wobbling a little.

'You could have rung him up a bit more. Invited him down.' She was trying to pick a fight with him. 'He was your friend, not mine. He was your *best friend.*'

It sounded like an accusation. He enjoyed another brief flash of anger and considered letting go of her arm and just leaving her here. Letting her find her own way back to the hotel. She was an adult. He had no obligation to her.

'He told me,' he said quietly. He was facing her

85

now, their faces very close, and although it was still noisy and she was still crying, making annoying little high-pitched sounds on the in-breath, as if she wanted not only him but everyone else in the bar to know that she was crying, he was almost certain that she had heard him and was pretending she hadn't.

He kept a tight hold of her arm and pulled her along beside him, through the endless crowd of the pub and towards the doors. He was not looking forward to getting her down the stairs and through the smoking crowd but knew that once they were out into the fresh air she would settle down. And the hotel was almost in sight.

'He felt bad about it. He told me. When I was here for Lila. He said.'

He looked at her face, her head lolling a little against his shoulder. They were at the door now and he opened it with one hand, keeping the other tight around her shoulders and clinging on to her. He was not feeling so steady himself.

'What did he say?'

'He said you'd been pissed and depressed and he'd taken advantage of you and he'd not been able to stop feeling terrible about it. He said he was worried about you. He said he thought you were deeply unhappy and I should see if I could get you to go to the doctor.'

'He told you all that?'

She won't remember. Won't remember this.

'He did. He was a real fucking saint about it.'

She laughed at this. And he wanted to laugh too. He could have done. Could have laughed and the pair of them could have gone back into the pub and ordered more whisky. Set about destroying the hours they had just lived through. Could it work like that? A blackout drunk? Could they bring it on, and so take everything back?

'He didn't take advantage,' she said dully.

'Were you trying to get pregnant?'

She shrugged. 'I don't know what I was doing. Have you never done anything and had no idea at all – none whatsoever – why you've done it?'

He considered this. He could be reckless now, and so, spurred on by the booze warming him up and making his face and throat hot, and not being able to tell if what he felt was anger or just more sadism or the final relief of surrender, he let himself be reckless.

'We can go to the doctor if you want to. The clinic. It's obviously me. I'll get a test. Fuck it.'

'It's thousands of pounds,' she said immediately,

and she sounded childlike – or was faking sounding childlike. She probably had the brochure for the clinic in her handbag. 'It's the house money.'

He wasn't fooled. She wasn't crying now. She'd responded too quickly, too eagerly, to be as out of it as she seemed.

'Yes,' he said. 'I know.'

Now they were out and down the steps and the smell of cigarette smoke was thick and sharp in the air, and it was much colder than it was an hour ago. He took off his jacket and put it around her shoulders – they'd have to ring around and find her coat in the morning, he supposed – and they crossed the road and walked shakily together towards the Premier Inn. She kept asking him if he meant it and he didn't answer her.

The hotel appeared as they rounded the corner: it was new, red-brick and glass, and ugly. There was a row of takeaway shops nearby, but out of sight, and he smelled garlic and fat and vinegar and fried chicken and his mouth watered. Maybe they could . . . He had a vision of them sitting on a bench somewhere, sharing a polystyrene clamshell of chips. For old time's sake. It would be nice, that: to finish off the night properly, like they did when they were younger. To find a way to put all the years since they'd left aside and come home, even if it was just for tonight.

He was about to suggest it, but there was the hotel: the sign for it leaked purple light onto the pavement and they crossed the empty road without waiting for the light to change.

PREMIER INN

AS THEY WENT up in the lift, which smelled like dirty carpets and perfume, she suddenly felt very sick. She rested her forehead on the mirrored wall, which she expected to be cool, but wasn't.

He was going to want her to say something, and she had been preparing her explanation for nearly a year: she'd been living with the mental effort of pushing this terrible thing downwards, below her thoughts, or of heaving it upwards and playing with the temptation of getting it into the light. She expected some type of relief. Of sitting humbly on their IKEA settee while he smashed glasses and broke the Nutribullet (why that, she doesn't know – but the fantasy was always specific on that point), and she would cry a bit, but also enjoy, at last, the heat of his jealousy, which would feel, finally, and indisputably, like love. And when that happened she could stop all this – all this effort – and just come to rest with him. It wouldn't be *settling*. It would be settling down. Were those things different?

The room they'd booked was right at the top of the hotel and the lift took a minute or so to finish its journey upwards. Her forehead had smudged the mirror. She swiped at it without registering her own reflection. He stood behind her, his hands around her waist for a moment.

'Are you all right?' she asked.

'Let's just get into the room.'

There was a little skip then – a jump in the tape – and now she was leaning against a wall in an endless corridor, a glowing fire escape light at the end. She watched him fumble with the key card – a white plastic thing instead of a key. He needed to slide it in and out of the slot quickly, and wait for the green light to show before he tried the handle – simple enough, but it took him a couple of tries to get right.

She kicked off her shoes. The carpet was thick and soft and she wiggled her toes, then the door was open and she rushed past him into the room and dropped her shoes on the floor, threw herself onto the bed, then regretted it, feeling all the drinks she'd had that night slosh around in her stomach.

'Home at last,' she said, full of fake cheerfulness. She was sober enough to know that she sounded drunk. 'I wonder what our lottery winners are doing? Do you think they're here too? Both still in one piece?'

He won't play with her. He was over by the window, inspecting the contents of the desk drawers, the little tray with the kettle, cups and saucers, the tea and coffee things. He liked hotels: always managed to make a strange room feel entirely his own within five minutes of getting into it. She marvelled at how he did it: some complex process of touching, taking possession of, and slightly rearranging every object in the place. She, on the other hand, only felt the ghosts of all the hands that had lifted the kettle, the strangeness of the hotel chains' bedrooms all looking precisely the same, the whispering echo of every stranger's head that had lain on her pillow. There was a card with a room service menu and he picked it up, looked at his watch hopefully, then let it fall.

'Is there a bath?'

He went to check. His voice echoed out of the tiny bathroom. 'Nope. Just a shower.'

She turned on the bed. She should take her dress off or she should talk to him, but the room around her was tilting and she could still feel the noise of the last pub thrumming in her ears. She closed her eyes. Sleep was already coming. And behind it – always pressing itself in around the edges – a greater weariness. A kind of grief. A loss too big to feel. She could think of babies – future babies riding high in three-wheeled prams and growing into shoes and school uniforms and bicycles and football games and nativity plays. All that. But the baby that had been lost – the wrong one – could not be considered.

The fan in the bathroom was whirring and she felt the vibration of it in her eyeballs and sternum. She wouldn't vomit and she wouldn't cry any more, if she could just sleep now.

When he came out of the bathroom, having un-wrapped a plastic beaker and filled it with water for her, she was already asleep. He untucked the duvet and tried to arrange it around her. Her make-up was spread over her face: now she looked like she'd been at a funeral. She did not cry when the pregnancy ended in a mess of blood and mucus down the toilet only four days after her first scan.

There had been a vicar or a priest of some kind talking about Simon's bike, his love of the outdoors, the way he had cared for his mother – and while this saintly stranger was eulogised he had experimented with the idea of letting go, or putting down. An idea, the acting out of which he did not believe himself to be fully capable. In theory then, what would it be like, if he did that?

He tried to imagine the helmet-cam footage: a tilting panorama of road and sky, tumbling. Simon would have known what was coming. Known in those final airborne seconds what was on its way. He should feel some satisfaction about that, if he was a proper bastard, if he really was angry. But he didn't. He sighed and put the water within arm's reach on her nightstand. He wished it hadn't happened. All of it. That was all.

The curtains were closed: they were heavy, and with difficulty he opened them, then pulled aside the filmy gauze behind them that hung there for privacy. He'd lost all sense of direction. In the glass, he saw nothing other than his own dark shape and the room's mirror laid out behind him, so he crossed the room, turned out the light and returned.

They were on the top floor, so he was half expecting a view of the town – past the shopping centre and over the accountants' and solicitors' offices in the big old pretty houses around Winkley Square, and the square itself, a little green bowl with trees and benches and the grass at the concave centre of it always boggy. The railings. He imagined the railings; now and again a bike chained to them missing one day its front wheel, the next, its back. Saddle and handlebars the last to go, until there's only a D-lock and a rusting, stripped frame. Beyond that he'd see the park – it would be a puddle of darkness now – just an inky spread spooning the river, but on the nearest side of the river, the north side, there was a wide lane flanked with newly planted trees and lamps. It used to be a green tunnel of old horse chestnut trees whose branches would meet overhead and throw green-veined shadows onto the root-cracked tarmac in the summer. But the city did it up. Improved it. Perhaps the trees had been too old to stand safely, or had contracted some disease.

They'd looked, the two of them, out of the train window as it crossed the final bridge over the park on the way into the station that morning, and had been surprised to see the avenue cleared and the tunnel gone, the walkway recovered and neatened up. The council had obviously made other improvements to the park: the old bandstand converted into a fancy pavilion café. The loss of the old trees – that green tunnel – had provoked a feeling in him a little like grief.

A memory surfaced: Si and a few of the others. There had been bottles of cider and someone had a guitar. Someone else had one of those circus toys that involved balancing and tossing a top onto a piece of string held taut and manipulated between two sticks. Had she been there with him? He could easily picture her in a black and purple T-shirt, a denim jacket. She used to have a backpack covered in patches. He remembered that, and so he puts her there, sitting with the rest of them. Sarah too. Helen. And others, peripheral others whose names he had lost but whose faces he pretended he could remember. Was he re-membering a particular day, or just an accretion of days?

There was a vagueness to the memory. He wasn't thinking of an event, just pasting together a jumble of fragments – the way they used to spend their time before they all left home. The way things tended to be.

In the scene he created they were all there on the old green bandstand, where the pavilion is now, with its Scandinavian pine and glass curves, modern and improved and out of place. He painted the old one back in: the dark and lime green paint, the graffiti, the way the metal would heat up where the sun hit it and become too hot to sit on. Mark was there too, being sent out of the park to the nearest shop to get sweets and cigarettes and pop and crisps, because he was the youngest and always had his bike with him and because he wouldn't say no to them. Mark turned and waved. Si said something clever, and the rest of them jeered approvingly.

In this memory, he is making tiny cigarettes with a pouch of dry tobacco and rolling papers, and passing them around. He passes one of them to her where she's sitting cross-legged. (Did she have a book? Was it a book she was reading? Was she there? He'll put her there, all the same – he'll say this was the day that they met, or the day that they first noticed each other properly. That's what he'll say.) There's a moment where she looks up from her lap and takes the cigarette from him and scowls her thanks and everything is contained in that moment, and only afterwards does he realise that she doesn't smoke, but she's kept the rollie tucked behind her ear all afternoon.

He cherished this not-quite-memory – not because their lives were so brilliant then (what he remembered more reliably was the boredom – the constant, weary-ing wait for someone to turn up or something to happen), but because their lives had not begun yet, and all the mistakes they were going to make were still in front of them, only dimly imagined. Was this home? Was this the moment he was always trying to travel back to? That moment when he passed her the cigarette and, frowning, she took it, because she didn't want it but she wanted him? He felt his grip on his past – on this entire city – loosen a little. *I have arrived.* The words floated up at him. He'd read them somewhere today, he thought, but he couldn't remember where.

They would have to come up with excuses for work. He cupped his hands around his eyes and moved his face to the glass, hoping for the park and the slow brown slopping of the river, wide and shal-low at this point, and the old tram bridge, the rails painted white, and all of it, all of it then and now, but as his eyes adjusted and his nose pressed against the glass, he laughed out loud as he realised what he was seeing. Only the backside of another tall building, and an almost empty car park, lit by the steady orange glow of the city lights. He tried to find his bearings, staggered a little as he stepped backwards into the chair near the desk, and laughed again – mainly at himself. The park and the rest of it would be there, sitting there in the dark quite happily without him, but he couldn't see it and was stupid to think otherwise.

He had woken her. She turned in the bed and tugged at an awkward corner of the duvet, trying to wrap it around herself.

'Sorry.'

She sat up and rubbed her hands over her face. 'Are we home yet?' she said, not quite awake.

'Sorry. That was me.'

He was not just apologising for waking her.

'I don't feel well.'

'You won't do. Try to get some sleep,' he said, and turned back to the window to grin at his view. He heard her get out of the bed. He listened to her sigh and reach for the plastic beaker. Heard the water click down her throat. He does not turn to her.

She was too hot. Her dress was creased and twisted and she struggled to reach the zip. He was still standing with his back to her, but she touched his elbow and turned and he understood what she wanted without her needing to ask. He unzipped it and held the beaker while she stepped out of the dress.

'What time is it?'

'Really late.'

She groaned. Took back the beaker and gulped down the rest of the water. She felt him next to her, his warmth and the faint smell of sweat and cigarettes – making its way across the space between them. In the silence she waited, and he turned to her, as she knew, or hoped, he finally would, and put his hand against her chest, searching out her heartbeat. She waited for him to find it, enjoying the weight and heat of his palm against her.

'Still alive?' she asked, smiling.

'You'll wish you weren't in the morning.'

'You kept your recording. The heart.' She heard herself slurring slightly, and tried not to, tried to rephrase her sentence, but he nodded and she saw he had understood what she'd meant.

'Of course I kept it.'

'Even though . . . ?

'Yes.' He tapped her collarbone lightly with his index finger. It's what he always does when she's upset: he says it puts her to sleep.

'Come to bed now,' she said, putting down the beaker and flopping gently back down against the pillows.

He stood over the bed, as if he was making a

decision. As if he was mulling over whether to get in, whether to stay in the hotel, whether to go back with her to London. As if all of those decisions hadn't already been made. As if he had anywhere else to go. He knew that in the morning they would wake late and not be able to manage the greasy all-you-can-eat breakfast that came with the price of the room. They would put their dirty clothes back on and travel down to London together – one of them going home, the other leaving home behind them – tucking the conversations had during their drinking hours away. He knew that their final destination still lay ahead of them.

By the time he'd taken his trousers off she was asleep again. He joined her.

JUDAS!

Benjamin Webster

BENJAMIN WEBSTER received the Northern Writers' Award for fiction in 2016. Born in Lancashire and now living in Yorkshire, *JUDAS!* is his first published work.

For all the Bees
BW

1. THESE DAYS

HE KNEW MANCHESTER better than most. The city had long since seeped into his bones. The old cotton mills and factories held his heart in a brown-brick cage, and the plumes from the chimneys filled his lungs. He'd spent so long there that it was as much a part of him as his own weakening frame and thinning skin. The people may have changed, their lines deepening or their faces new. The awnings and signage may have changed, too. Even the skyline was altered from time to time: local boys and overseas investors announcing their arrival by rewriting the sky and repainting the stars that hummed just beyond the soupy glow of the street lights. But the city, the city was the same. Its heart beat far down below the concrete streets, where no one could get to it, no matter how far they dug down and built up, how much money they spent altering its face and erasing its past.

The real heart of Manchester beat in a slice of the city carved out by Peter Street and Deansgate. The Romans used it as a thoroughfare before the Anglo-Saxons turned up, chased them off and gave it a new name. A road was then built to connect it to the river, then a quay was built in the eighteenth century and the industrialisation of the city began.

But it wasn't the city's heart he was looking for.

The place where he found himself, that day and most, remained fields for years after Manchester's birth. That was where the city had found its voice; that was where it had chosen to communicate with him. From there you could have observed the child of Manchester growing, chewing up the land and getting stronger. During those baby steps, power still lay in the rural areas: the Corn Laws kept the price of grain high, making famine and unemployment rife in towns and cities. This caused Manchester's dispossessed to march, gathering on a scruff of croft called St Peter's Field. There they were charged by cavalrymen and attacked with bayonets. Over ten perished and hundreds more were injured in the resulting riots that stretched into the next day.

The Free Trade Hall was constructed to commemorate the repeal of the Corn Laws a few years later. Its sturdy arches and pillars sheltered ornately crafted spandrels carrying the names of the other Lancashire towns that stood in defiance, while a delicate frieze of tympana above paid tribute to the arts, free trade and commerce. It was brave, bold and stoic but also ornate, beautiful and eccentric. It was Manchester in two sturdy storeys.

In later years it became a live music venue. He'd first encountered the Free Trade Hall back in the 1970s when he sat outside all night trying to get tickets to see The Rolling Stones perform a final farewell to the UK before they became tax exiles on Main Street. Both shows had completely sold out by the time he got to the front of the queue, leaving him to stumble empty-handed into the morning, kicking away the detritus left by more satisfied fans.

He came back the morning after and was still returning years later. If anyone would have stopped to speak to him in the years in between, they might have put it down to his first real taste of disappointment: a behavioural loop he couldn't break free from, the portrait of a long and sorry life started in the muted grey tones of that empty morning. But they would have had to speak to him to do that, and no one ever did – even the city seemed reluctant since his first communion.

That didn't stop him from trying. He was a holey-soled pilgrim on a path to enlightenment; his road led not to Damascus but Peter Street, where he would plant his roots and wait for the city to water him.

He slipped a square piece of cardboard from inside his jacket and rolled it out onto the pavement. Then he placed his back against the wall and lowered himself down as his legs began their chorus of protest (though by now they knew he wasn't going to listen; their actions were as much a habit as his). He watched people, their eyes glancing off blistering fly-posters outside the museum, their bodies folded into chairs behind tall panes of glass, gazing at the glowing black mirrors in their palms. He saw them in solitary strands on crowded tram platforms like stray blades of grass, or chasing the bright lights in spirited packs as the light dimmed over St Peter's Square. But they weren't his concern. And, thankfully, he wasn't theirs.

The setting for his first communion was non-descript: just a thin cobbled vein that swallowed the thrum and the noise of the thoroughfare to such an extent that passing through wasn't unlike being submerged in a tepid bath of murky water. Afterwards he had to be told that the cyclist had peeled off the road, darted between two bollards and struck him at high speed, otherwise he would have woken from his first visit with nothing but a ringing in his ears, a crumpled five-pound note in his hand, a large purple lump rising like a fried egg on his forehead and the not insignificant knowledge that his life was forever changed.

The walls helped him up as the stones and bricks swirled around his periphery. He looked down at his old shoes then back up to see concerned eyes loom tightly into his face. Her perfume smelled of honey and orange. Her voice was nothing but a whisper under the blood in his ears. "E left you a fiver,' she said, before using 'snide' as a bridge and 'prick' as a full stop. He opened his palm to see a crumpled plasticky portrait of Winston Churchill looking as rough as he felt. 'You all right, love?' He nodded and walked away slowly. 'You were out for a time.'

He stumbled to a café, ordered a cup of tea, said goodbye to Winston and hello to five dull coins that gave an unusual heft and purpose to his pockets. The waking city gave way to a cup of weak tea as he held his splitting head in his hands. Through the pounding of his heart and the coursing of his blood and the rising steam that warmed the end of his nose and cheeks, he climbed back up into his head and replayed the memories that had swallowed him while his body covered a small space on Southmill Street.

Four rows back in a large dark hall. He could hear the shallow breathing of hundreds, or thousands, of others around him and up on the balconies. The anticipation was only slightly less audible; it prompted a surge of nervous electricity somewhere below his balls. A single spotlight turned on, and a small man in a thick grey suit walked on the stage to loud applause, an acoustic guitar in his clutch and a harmonica around his neck. His fingers flicked over the strings and stilled the claps. He sang a song over a gentle melody. He didn't know it then (but he would hear it countless times later). He knew Bob Dylan, but he wouldn't have called himself a fan.

The performance continued: one man and two instruments. Each song welcomed at the finish line by warm applause and something like relief bubbling just underneath. 'Mr. Tambourine Man' was played five songs in. It was the only one he knew. He could feel the hairs rise under his neat clothes. He looked down and saw young hands placed on knees that didn't look like his. He looked up at the chandeliers hanging in the shadows, small fragments of light catching the reflection from the stage. 'Thank you,' he whispered into the silence, and he smiled widely. A young girl turned and saw him and smiled right back. 'Thank you very much.'

He closed his eyes.

''E left you a fiver,' said the voice. The light outside hurt his eyes. Something had collided with him. 'Snide prick,' she said. A cyclist hit him, a cyclist and so much more. 'You all right, love?' she asked as he hurried away.

That was the first and only time the city had spoken to him. How long had it been? Weeks? Months? Manchester only really had two seasons, both of which involved consistent but varying degrees of rainfall, so the passing of time was hard to measure. The memories of that night didn't seem to falter, however, and sometime later, as the fried egg was digested by his skin and the coins were long since lost to his pockets, he began to try and recreate the event that led him to that night, to the concert which he was certain had taken place in The Free Trade Hall sometime in the 1960s.

The first step was to try and self-administer mild

concussion. Blighted, shamed and taunted by the projections playing on the inside of his eyelids, he walked slowly down Watson Street towards the old G-Mex Centre. His feet stopped on the pavement between a restaurant and a casino. Canola oil and the lemony scent of hot Sichuan pepper chased away the numbness on his face, but were in turn shooed off by a pother of cigar smoke. It seemed to be trying to escape the brash declarations of a gaggle of swaying men wrapped in thin dark suits, proudly announcing their intent to chase the night away from the blackjack tables.

A watery pink eye caught his, as if it had seen the thoughts inside and not the sad and shabby man over the dark side of the street that incubated them. He turned quickly and dipped into the shadows hung from a wide doorway. The men flicked their cigar nubs at some wheelie bins before heading through the glass doors. He slunk out like an alley cat and moved towards the two small indentations sunk in the cobbled road. He fanned his long coat, folded it over his chest and lay down on his side, his right temple covering one of the shallow holes.

And he waited.

He'd never seen the automatic traffic bollards rise

on Watson Street but once spent the best part of a summer's afternoon pondering the front end of a Ford Focus skewered by the ones on Market Street. He reasoned that they'd do a decent job of removing him from his tether of consciousness for a short while.

A few uneventful minutes chased the fire from the cigar embers and slowly pushed his eyelids together. His knees and chest moved closer, and he folded in on himself and soon fell into a slumber in the centre of the road. The passing of time was carried by dreamless sleep. When he awoke he would not feel rested or satiated; the city's voice would be thinner and more distant, yet he would be more determined to find it and more upset that so far he had failed.

His eyes opened by the wheelie bins. He had a black suit jacket folded neatly under his head. The twin shadows of two risen traffic bollards formed a dismissive V sign in the sallow morning light; it stretched over the road towards his sore eyes. Ignoring the cries of ignominy from his bones, he rolled onto his front and slowly pushed himself to his knees. His fingers prodded the pillowy jacket like it might stir and wake too. Instead it coughed a few loose casino chips onto the cobbles. He scooped them up and stumbled away, looking to reunite the jacket with its owner, unable to recognise an act of charity even in its most drunkenly obvious form.

He bartered a cup of tea at the taxi drivers' café two streets away – a safe enough distance for him to try and reassemble his head while the smell of sizzling bacon seeped into his hair and clothes, like the cold on his back and the hollow disappointment getting comfy in his bones. He was a ghost in the modern world, offering little but a remembrance of the past to anyone who witnessed him. Yet it seemed determined to keep him there. And all the while the space between where he was and where he wanted to be stretched like bubblegum. The city could be cruel sometimes.

2. EVER FALLEN IN LOVE . . .

WHAT BECAME OF The Free Trade Hall, brick-built bastion of freedom and long-standing testament to the North's spirit of justice and rebellion? After hosting Dickens and Churchill, housing the Hallé orchestra, being almost vaporised in the Christmas Blitz of 1940, then being slowly reborn in time to birth Manchester's musical renaissance in the 1970s. After hosting the Dalai Lama and Oscar Wilde (unfortunately, not on the same bill), after surviving bombs and decades of rain and pigeon shit, it was eventually betrayed by the city that raised it, left to ruin and sold off to a development consortium. Their grand vision was for the hall to add gravitas to a contemporary temporary urban habitation experience. You too could be Bob Dylan but with free Wi-Fi and a bird's-eye view of the city's changing skyline above the small twinkling

115

street lights and the ants scurrying to the tram platforms below.

He wasn't aware of a disconnect between free trade and commerce when he awoke that morning, at least until he returned to his stoop under the protective wing of the arches. 'You can't be here, mate.' It sounded like just another series of disassociated words rising above the noise on Peter Street; not for his ears, but he tended to catch them from time to time. 'Mate,' it said. 'Mate,' it said. 'Mate!' it shouted. He'd never seen someone else's shoes stand still for so long. They were aquamarine, so bright, so new-looking. The brogues tilted like they were praying, small folds in the leather. A young black man in a powder blue suit stooped to his eyeline, keeping a safe space in between. 'You need to leave,' he said, his voice dropping octaves.

'Free country,' he replied.

The man laughed. 'Yeah? When was the last time you checked?'

His skills of conversation had lain dormant for far too long – and weren't too well-honed when he last used them. This conversation was already going on far too long. 'How much?' he asked.

'Mate, you don't have enough. Trust me. The

only reason they let me through those doors is because I work here.' He reached into the jacket pocket and scooped out a pile of plastic chips. The man smiled. 'Look, *James Bond*, even if you had enough it wouldn't *be* enough, you know what I'm saying?'

He looked west. That road led to the River Irwell and had done since the times of the Romans. East went past the library, turned into Oxford Road and crossed a narrow stretch of the River Medlock. He knew the buildings and the roads and the alleys; he knew the sun patterns and the shadows; where the rain gathered, where to avoid walking on the pavements when it did. The times of the trains and the buses, he knew it all like he was privy to the city's most intimate moments and movements. He'd been everywhere, and he knew that there was nowhere else for him to go.

The young man sighed and looked through the long glass doors of the hotel. 'Come on, mate,' he whispered. 'Do me a favour. My boss has already seen his arse today. I'm not normally like this. Really, I'm not. Just today. Please.'

Marcus. That's what his name badge said. The accompanying photo saw him carry a smile that seemed wider than his face. The real version above was scowling at him for the benefit of whoever was looking through the glass doors. His eyes told a different story, though; they were too wide and too wet, like a dog when it just wants to go outside and run about for a bit. Not a big ask. He wasn't going to get what he wanted by being accommodating, but, clearly, he wasn't going to get what he wanted at all.

'Do you know what this place was, Marcus?' he asked the young man, who looked puzzled for a second until he glanced down at his badge, shook his head and smiled in surprise at being outwitted.

'Free Trade Hall,' he replied. 'My dad said he saw Bowie here in the seventies.'

He nodded. 'And before that?'

'I was born in the eighties,' Marcus said. 'There was no before that.'

'Freedom from oppression,' he said. 'It was built as a reminder to anyone who might come here and tell us what to do that others have tried and failed. It was a place of ideas and inspiration. It was where the city found its voice.' It was the longest he'd spoken in some years. He was surprised by how easy it was to manifest the words outside of his head.

'And then they flogged it off and turned it into

a hotel. I guess free trade is a double-ended sword, eh? Listen, mate, I don't need you explaining oppression to me, and if I wanted a history lesson I'd be in college. But I'm working here, and as much as it's not for me, it's all I've got going on at the moment. So are you going to help or what?' His arm slipped away from his shirt cuff and he reached down an open palm.

He decided to acquiesce. The city was nearly 2,000 years old; it wasn't going anywhere. What was one day between friends? He could try and walk his headache off, or visit that big stone kidney bean outside the Bridgewater Hall and try to figure out what it was for. He reached up with his hand.

And that's when they met.

Three rows back in a large dark hall. The audience were making a noise of being quiet. He knew this anticipation. He knew what was coming. He felt the electricity again, above his ...

Here is Bob Dylan. Here is his grey suit and his guitar and his harmonica. See how he uses them to silence the applause. See his hands skimming the strings. Watch him breathe. Hear him sing ...

The song is familiar now (he will later know it

as 'She Belongs to Me') but the view isn't. He looks around. The wooden hall in the thin glow radiating from the spotlight is just like he remembered. He glances up at the chandeliers and watches their residual sparkle for so long that he won't be able to remember the song ending and the next one beginning.

It is sometime during this spell that he realises he is no longer himself, nor the himself he was the last time he visited. He looks down at his body and realises that his hands are smaller and more beautiful and that he is wearing a black pencil skirt and suede knee-high boots. He turns to the seat behind him as 'Mr. Tambourine Man' begins. He sees a young man. His eyes aren't on Bob Dylan. They are on him. They are glazed and wet as tears gather at the bottom of his eyes. And though the man he sees is from a different time and place, he knows that he is carrying the man from the hotel inside him like one of those Russian dolls. He smiles at Marcus, in part through vindictive pleasure at his discomfort, but mostly in relief, that he made it back and that someone is here to witness his miracle. He holds out a hand to try and soothe his panic, stopping only briefly to ponder the colour of his nails. The man slowly raises a shaking hand in return as sweat rills off his face. Their hands meet, and he feels something like electricity from the boy's palms.

3. TEMPTATION

IT WASN'T TOO surprising to see clouds gathering above that day. Manchester is a place of constant change – witness the city's bees, so named for their productivity, gathering in stadiums instead of cotton mills – but if there's one main constant, it's the wet weather. If you see someone walking round the city without a brolly then they've either been in Manchester too long or not long enough (Marcus himself was well used to having a wet neck). It still struck him as strange that he had never experienced light so vivid. The blue from his shoes seemed like it might make his eyes pop. Even the brown stone of the hotel seemed to thrum with a bright intensity. It even hurt to look at the man sat opposite him, though he looked like a new and particularly uninspiring shade of grey. Life had dropped a few frames, maybe even skipped a reel.

As his head seemed to join him in the present a few seconds later, he realised he was holding the hand of the man he'd been tasked with getting rid of. 'What the fuck, man. Get off!' The man tried to hush him. 'What was that? Did you spike me? What the fuck? What the fuck!' He started breathing on his shoes as the colours dialled down.

'I was there,' the man said. His eyes were too wide, too lit. He knew it was true. 'That was me,' the man said with pride. He jabbed a thumb towards the inside of the hotel. 'In there.'

There were few witnesses to his entrance into the Free Trade Hall. This was an epochal, some might even say religious, event that many of the local glitterati might later claim to have witnessed (not unlike that night in 1976 when thousands claimed to have seen the Sex Pistols play a venue that held 150 at best). There was Krysia manning the long reception desk. She cupped a phone to her ear as she locked down rooms for a block booking, and the need to get it right was greater than putting a face to the man her friend Marcus was escorting. So much so that their manager, normally the kind to detect a loose hair on a carpet, was too busy craning his neck in a futile attempt to hear the droning voice on the far end to notice. Likewise, the couple waiting for their taxi in the foyer picked up nothing but the stray scent of rain on the air and a musty smell of clothing that had been in the cupboard for far too long.

But if any of them had looked up they would have seen a man collecting wonder with his eyes.

The Free Trade Hall had been painted and gentrified; its eccentricities had been worn down and layered over with the kind of strange modern art accoutrements you buy by the yard. But it was still *there*. He felt a memory of his last visit, however long that had been. Both minutes and decades, he supposed. No amount of glass, strange art and soft furnishings could dilute the power of the place.

He was steered to a door past the long shiny reception desk and walked to a bar that seemed to be made entirely of wood and glass. Huge granite heads peered out of dimly lit alcoves. 'Sit,' Marcus offered, sternly. He was working hard to regain composure. The quickstep squeak of his brogues on marble gave way to gentle piano music. A bartender polished glass and restocked the see-through fridges, unaware or unconcerned by the man's presence. He closed his eyes and held his breath till his lungs ached and his head spun unto the point of collapse. The lightness dimmed as his breath became more settled, and he realised what he would need to venture back. The one thing he had managed to avoid so effortlessly was the one thing that would enable him to visit again. Here he was in the bowels of history. Surely here he would be able to travel back again. He needed Marcus. He needed to—

'Explain,' the returning Marcus commanded. He put a glass of water down in front of the man. 'What you did to me.'

'Sit down,' he invited. Marcus made extra effort to appear like he was just about to sit down anyway. His eyes were only open a hair's breadth and did not move off the man, who was reaching out with a welcoming hand.

'Keep them to yourself,' Marcus ordered with a little too much volume. The barman turned his eyes their way. Marcus tried to ignore him but lowered his volume all the same. 'Why shouldn't I just kick you out?'

'Because you invited me in,' the man said. He took a quick sip of water. Marcus noted his eyes moving over the walls like explorers' lamps. Everywhere they pointed seemed to offer new information on some unknown civilisation. Yet they absorbed little, as if he was disappointed by what he found. He was right about Marcus, too; he was beholden to his curiosity, to his desire for something, anything different to *this*. Witness the fact that the man he was tasked with removing was now sat down at his invitation, drinking water he had provided. 'This place deserves better,' the man said.

'Why'd you say that?'

'Great minds used to come here to share ideas. Music was performed, people were inspired and lives were changed. What's it got now?'

'Conference facilities and a piano player,' Marcus replied with a half-hollow heart. He couldn't find it in himself to disagree with the man entirely. His dad once told him what a place this was when he was young. It was one of the few vivid memories of him that he still carried.

'Does your old man still visit here then?'

'He doesn't get out much,' Marcus said. 'Hard to when you're wearing six feet of dirt.' He pressed his fingers to his temples and closed his eyes, expecting to open them again and see an empty chair and a full glass of water; the man no more than a sore pulse beating in his head. But there he still was: a living headache left on a carved wooden seat. 'What did you do to me?' Marcus asked the man. 'Is it like hypnosis?'

'I didn't hypnotise you,' the man said. 'This place did. It took me back to the 1960s, and then it took you back with me.'

'You're tapped.'

'Then so are you,' he said. 'You were four rows back. That's where I was first time. I was the girl in front of you on the second time. So we're either both mad or neither of us are.'

Marcus looked over at the barman and then tilted his head out to reception. 'I'd have to be mad to bring you in here, to be having this conversation. Look, mate, I'm sorry, but I can't do this. I have to get you out.'

'Let me stay,' the man said. 'I have money.' He dug quickly into the pockets of the black suit jacket and pulled out a pile of casino chips. A few slipped and spilled from the top, tapping and rolling over the marble floor. Marcus walked them down and brought them back.

'So you're *Rainman* now. OK. That makes sense. I get it.' Marcus folded his hands and cradled his chin. He looked at the loose stitching of the man's clothes.

His jacket lining was ripped, stuffing exposed like the ragged tear of an animal bite. 'Where do you live?'

The old man shrugged. 'In the city,' he muttered.

'In the streets?'

'In her hands,' he corrected.

Marcus looked down at his feet. He wasn't keen on aquamarine, and he often thought his powder blue suit made him look like a narrow tube of toothpaste. Not as often as he once did, but still . . . 'I'll find you somewhere to stay,' he said. 'Does that jacket fit you?'

The storage cupboard was located in the hotel's basement. It was a sorry and dark place that was fated to be a Roman-themed health club and spa.

If the Free Trade Hall was Manchester's reply to the Corn Laws, then this place, a cavernous room bearing stone grapes, ornate plaster wreaths and large plastic urns, was perhaps Italy's revenge on the Angles. Or was it the other way round? Either way, it struck him that the slighted would be well over it by the time he was used to sleeping with a ceiling over his head.

Freedom was an illusion, even down there. He had to keep the door closed during the day as workmen were on the other side, busying themselves looking busy. Their habitual sighs and groans were easy to detect, as was the heavy clomping of their boots when they fetched tea and baccy pouches, or underwent their sacred and lengthy ablutions. And when they occasionally plugged their power tools in – mainly for the benefit of those above ground – he almost wished he were somewhere else.

Almost.

Marcus told him that in twelve weeks they were already eight months behind schedule, and that his boss – mindful of bad reflections in a way that only a man who stands in front of tall panes of glass all day could be – had recently taken it upon himself to crack the whip. The foreman's response? 'Rome worren't built in a day worrit, cock.' After that the basement was a responsibility-free zone. The manager only paced the soft carpets and marble floors above, burying the thoughts of those under his feet like you might some ancient curse.

At night he was free to wander the halls in the bright arcs of the site lights. He would stare through the glass at the large empty pool. It was perhaps the only place his body could visit that still resembled the old Free Trade Hall. Sometime in the near future it would be inaccessible to the likes of him, but right now, it was his and his alone. That kept him mildly satiated. He hadn't been back to witness a performance since he'd brought his companion. And though Marcus seemed happy to assist him, by bringing him food and keeping a lookout so he could escape the smell of chlorine and fresh paint, his desire to revisit the events that bound them together was a little more oblique. It revealed itself on occasion: he would ask if everything was still *OK*. The emphasis on the last word, and the silence that followed, was clearly filled with desire, but so far he'd managed to bite his tongue and forgo the temptation to ask that simple question: 'Could we go back?'

He knew the next visit wasn't too far ahead. He'd been planning a special event and, until Marcus was ready to accept the invitation, he was happy to potter in the bowels of the hall, to run his fingers on the newly painted walls and try to absorb its past glories through some form of osmosis. His only concession was to wear that ill-fitting suit jacket when he did. He didn't mind; it almost made him feel like someone else.

There were many dates now filed in his head: 22 June 1969, 6 November 1971, 8 June that same year and 17 May 1966 (the date of Dylan's performance), each one like a greyhound in a trap. But it was 12 September in the present year that carried the most significance. The day slipped away with little muster, but the occurrence it contained was not unlike someone bringing a flame to meet a firework. And while the slow burn that followed would bring others into their orbit, it began in the inauspicious surrounds of an empty swimming pool with two men sat on upturned buckets eating from a bag of Chinese food.

He'd already learned not to eat prawn tails but still did so anyway, the same way anyone who'd known hunger might. Marcus had given up telling him. Who was he to say what he should eat, anyway? He didn't recognise half the stuff he gave to his stomach. So they ate in silence, but were sufficiently at ease in each other's company for that not to be a problem. Marcus never questioned why he allowed the man to stay here, beyond the basic idea of doing a good turn, and the man didn't seem to question it. All he'd really learned about him was that he loved Chinese food, something Marcus reciprocated. He'd had longer relationships built on less.

Marcus put the empty, oily containers back in the bag after their stomachs had surrendered to the food and pulled out two fortune cookies in thin silver wrappers. He tossed one to the man, who caught it and held it up until it glowed in the shallow glare of the pool lights. 'What's this?' he asked.

'Fortune cookie,' Marcus replied. He peeled back the wrapper and produced something like a deep-fried butterfly. The man did the same and was about to offer it to his mouth. 'Don't eat it,' Marcus said. 'Nobody eats them. There's a message in the middle.' He snapped the biscuit thing and pulled out a thin strip of paper. 'They tell your future,' he said. 'What's yours say?'

He broke the cookie's wings and pulled out the paper. He held it in front of his face and studied it intently, but the small black shapes made no sense.

'What's it say?' Marcus teased.

'What does yours say?' The man asked.

'YOU WILL GO ON A LONG JOURNEY,' Marcus replied in a monotone voice, smiling widely at the end. 'They say any old shite, really. If it told me where and when, then they might be onto something.' He braced his belly and belched. 'Excuse me. What about you?'

His eyes fed the words to his mouth, but his mind could not chew them. But his lips still moved, and by the time they had excreted '21 APRIL 1972', Marcus's smile was gone.

'That's the weirdest fortune cookie ever,' he said. 'Let me see.'

'You don't want to,' the man said.

'Let me see.'

'No.'

'Why not?' He stood up and knocked the plastic bucket onto its side. It rolled in a small circle. 'What's it mean?'

'Are you sure you want to know?'

'Yes. Stop being a knob.' Marcus reached slowly for the paper. The man gave it up with a smile. 'You're such a weirdo,' he said. The man grabbed his wrist with the other hand. And they left.

The world is ghosting. Everything has two images. They shake and bleed into each other. It's like TV static, only . . . real? The sound rises into a shrill hiss that sounds like someone shaking a bag of rattlesnakes playing the maracas. It descends until it sounds like the bag is in a bin filled with feathers. Despite that it's watchable in an 'I can't be arsed to change it and there's probably nothing on the other channel' kind of way.

The hall could take a few thousand. But they're fired up. They're ready. The stewards shake their heads. (*What new nonsense is this?*) Here are The Spiders. (*They pretend to be from Mars but guess what? They're from Hull.*) Marcus feels it now, a sensation like when you're falling or being chased by someone who wants to do you in. He feels it below his belly, which feels strangely empty.

The hotel was supposed to be a stopgap. That's what he'd told himself two years ago. He was just waiting for something. He was just waiting for inspiration. He was waiting for *him*. He was waiting for ... Ziggy Stardust?

The crowd loses its shit. His fear turns to excitement, to enormous possibility. He sees the young faces, all the pretty things, and wonders how much someone might want this, for a while, just a spell. There can't be more than a couple of hundred of them. They swarm the stage, so much love and so much energy. Were these better times? It makes him feel like they were, and he's not even a fan of Bowie, not like his dad was.

A door opens somewhere in his mind. The crowd shuffles Marcus as they bray and clamour for the Starman. Unfamiliar eyes catch the stage lights. *Come on*, the voice calls to him from afar, through the buzzing fog in his ears. The static rises in volume as his vision splits in two. He squeezes his head and closes his eyes. It hurts. Dancing limbs prod and poke him. No one would want this, he thinks. He tries to make it to the side, shuffling painfully through the crowd. His head is on fire.

He struggles to bring the world into clarity. The last times were so much easier. Why not now? The noise stops him from thinking clearly. The broken image of the handful of people around him in the circle makes his stomach fold. Everything else feels like breaking glass. He closes his eyes. It's all too much. Manchester isn't talking to him any more; it's screaming. The friendship he'd been kindling all these years, it feels like it's all over.

Then, like the final violent throes of a storm, the torture stops. The sound pours smoothly into his ears. He opens his eyes to the teenage boy next to him and witnesses someone undergoing religious reassignment with almost perfect clarity. Likewise, the collective fervour down in front of the stage becomes razor-sharp. He sees the preening, strutting figure on stage;

his audience enraptured, hanging on every word, completely malleable in his hands. It's mesmerising.

A teenage girl pilots her way through the crowd. He sees the world regain its keel for Marcus from above. She stops walking and looks up. He waves to her. The girl catches it and tilts her head down to acknowledge him. She teeters on her feet. Someone holds her, helps her up. Marcus receives his gift and he is here to witness it. The sorrow and regret have faded. He feels something else, something no one will ever feel. And he smiles down on him.

'Dad?' Marcus asks.

'You what?' the man shouts his reply and smiles. 'What are you on, love?'

It has to be his dad, Marcus thinks. How many Bowie fans could there be that look like him? How many here, tonight?

'Thought you were someone else,' he replies.

'Well, you're welcome,' his dad says. Marcus can do nothing but stare. His dad is younger than he is now. That's strange, but then he's getting to know strange now. The lines worn on his dad's brow aren't there. The grey hairs haven't appeared yet. His eyes are so bright, his shirt collars so big. He smiles, and from the smile that meets his he realises that he's probably not in the body of a scally, or any of the old firms his dad used to tell him about when mum was out of earshot (not that half of them would be seen dead there). Marcus turns away, wanting to absorb everything about this moment.

'Ziggy Stardust' starts up. It's like someone summoned a living snapshot of his childhood. He remembers peering over the wonky record player when his legs were tall enough. The stylus bounced like it was travelling slowly down a bumpy black road. He remembers the scratch, the static kicked up like loose pebbles. (*This is music, kidder. Forget that other stuff.*) He mouths the words as they fall from Bowie's lips.

'How'd you know this 'un?' his dad asks, so close that he almost chokes on the forgotten scent of English Leather aftershave. 'Not even out yet.'

Marcus shrugs and turns back to the stage. He watches his dad smile from the corner of his eyes. He feels a glimmer inside, a world of new possibilities opening. There's a hand on his shoulder. He slips away just as the crowd begin to carry the 'Leper Messiah' on their shoulders.

There were tears in his eyes when he opened them. He hadn't cried since he buried his old man. Even then he had to hide himself away from others looking to direct all their guilt and sympathy onto him, like he was a lightning conductor for their grief. He wouldn't let them see that he couldn't take it all those years ago, and he wouldn't then either.

He picked up the bags, climbed out the pool and walked. He wanted to say something to the man, but the words were hidden. He knew that his voice would have been too weak to carry them anyway.

The man just sat and watched with gladness and sympathy in his eyes. Even if he wanted to console the boy, he knew that he couldn't. Some things couldn't be tamed by putting your hands on them. Influence sometimes took time. And that's something he knew they had. He saw the future; he knew their miracle would return. He saw so far. He saw it all . . . and yet not.

There were other eyes on them that night, other eyes that would take them someplace else. They watched him retire to his cupboard before creeping back upstairs.

The city gave way to low-rise estates and green spaces that glowed sleepily under the street lights. Marcus watched the Heineken factory emerge slowly from the orange haze of the late night; its silver chimney like one of the fags his Uncle Reg smoked because he thought it made him look posh. He was dead too. But even when he was alive he wouldn't have been seen dead inside the Free Trade Hall, only venturing as far as The Reno or other local places where he wouldn't stick out. His aspirations didn't move from under the brewery's gaze. Not like his dad's. Not like his. But there he was, heading homewards. The past thirty minutes a blackout, those preceding them like a fever dream.

Some kids watched him from over the street. He kept his head down. Probably just looking out for his mum. Don't want trouble. He made a point of holding out his key. Hoped it looked like a key from over the way. He closed the door quietly and gently pushed his back against it while his heart thumped in his chest. There was laughter from out there. He pretended he was too frayed to care, but it felt like his heart was outside himself and everything hurt.

'That you, Marcus?'

'Yes, Mums,' he calls.

'Hungry, love?'

'Nah, all good. I'll see you in the morning, yeah?'

'Love you, Boy.'

'Love you.'

Just a few steps to the living room; felt like an age when he was a kid. He looked at the photos over the five-bar fire. The years were a blink. He saw his dad as he'd just seen him that night. Amazing what old cameras missed, though. The rest of his life followed in little snaps. Somewhere in the space between his dad had moved on. Marcus fanned through his dad's dusty records, slipping *Ziggy Stardust* out of the middle. The crackle sounded louder than the music. Didn't matter; he wanted to see it spin more than he needed to hear it. Besides, the studio mix lost a lot of Ziggy's rawness, his physical performance. Marcus collapsed on a kitchen chair and cried like he hadn't cried in years.

There was a knock on the door in the early hours. Marcus popped his head out and turned it up and down the street. No one had seen the crazy man on his doorstep. *That's good. Maybe he's not real.* He closed the door. More knocks. *Crazy man still on doorstep. Not good.*

'Shut the fuck up,' Marcus hissed. 'Mum's still sleeping.'

'I'm up, Marcus. You watch your mouth, Boy.' His

mum rolled to the door behind him and peered out into the hazy apricot yawn of the morning. 'Who's this?' she asked, her waking eyes slowly feeding her brain. Her son had done worse, had worse come to their door. She'd learnt to give him the benefit of the doubt, no matter how mean-looking, rough-looking or fragrant the visitor.

Marcus stepped out of the house and softly closed the door on his mum's curiosity. The morning was cold. It climbed down the back of his jacket and clung to his shoulders. He folded his arms and rolled on his feet. He tipped his head and beckoned for the man to join him on a small square patch of lawn, wet with dew spray, as the sun rose over the low houses.

'How'd you find me?'

'She told me,' the man answered; his eyes were just small slits pointed towards the rising sun.

'Krysia?'

'Her,' he said and beckoned widely with his hands, like even the idea of the city was too big to contain. Marcus smiled, shook his head and turned his eyes to his feet.

'Well, maybe she talks too much,' Marcus said. 'No secrets in the city, yeah?'

The man stared back at the sun, then turned back

to Marcus and held out a small white ribbon of paper that flickered gently in the air.

His eyes moved between the man and the paper. But the invitation was too great, his curiosity, too heavy. Marcus reached out and whipped the paper from the man's fingers. The message, block-printed on a slim piece of paper, simply stated: TWO DAYS FROM NOW TOMORROW WILL BE YESTER-DAY.

'No secrets,' he said, then turned coat and started back towards the city like the Deansgate tower had him in its gravitational pull. Marcus felt something too. A direction. A purpose. It was something that hadn't been in his skin since his college days.

'I'm coming with you,' he called, kicking himself for shouting but feeling like he had a tiger on his tails.

'There's time,' the man said. He walked slowly back to Peter Street and knew that the sun would soon look upon him. It would be a good day.

4. THE MASTERPLAN

NEW BUSINESS FUNDAMENTALS: keep your over-heads low and your incomes high. If they meet there might be a kink in your business plan that needs some finessing. If they swap places then something more drastic is required: a refined strategy, the trimming of your outgoings. If they like their new positions, and seem fixed on not budging, then get used to the taste of tinned food.

The first part was easy; the roof over their head and the light and the warm air on their skin were not only being paid for by someone else, but Marcus was being financially gratified for the pleasure of their company. The second part was easy in theory. Who wouldn't want to travel back in time, to be someone else, to see the greatest of Manchester's musical offerings in the hallowed surroundings of the Free Trade Hall? But how to find them? What to charge?

Was it safe, legal, even possible? Knowing your target audience was something else entirely. Marcus favoured high-earners, but his recent experience had put an unwelcome spiritual bent on proceedings, and try as he might he couldn't quite square that circle. It was troubling.

'They should pay something,' the man said. 'A token.' The novelty of not seeing the stars was wearing off. Even behind its plastic housing he could smell the bleach and the chlorine. The noise of the workmen, in their long periods of inaction, was driving him to distraction. He may have been in the foundations of his temple, but it was hard to communicate with all the extraneous bobbins around. Even the Roman stylings, which he'd previously found a charming reminder of the city's ancient past, were starting to wear thin. Like the clothes on his back and the hairs on his head.

'A token,' Marcus repeated with mild disbelief. The numbers on the balance sheets in front of his eyes resembled little scurrying ants that crawled over the paper in search of greater sustenance. 'We need investment,' he said. 'Something to buy us time.' He was also surprised that the man didn't disagree. Instead he reached into his crumpled black dinner jacket and scooped out the pile of plastic casino chips. It was like everything he kept in his pockets, just dreams. And yet...

'You only had nine days left on these chips, Mr Hallenhoofer. I can only imagine what you've been doing since,' the lady at the desk said with a glint in her eye as a wry smile slipped past her cheeks. She seemed to believe the story, a strange thing in itself, as the look of him – a too-tight black jacket that seemed to be strangling his torso, wiry black stubble that made him resemble both a chimney sweep and his brush, and distant eyes lost in dark sockets – suggested that he was lucky to remember his name, let alone where to collect his blackjack winnings.

Mr Hallenhoofer. As fake names go, it was both generally memorable and yet specifically not. Marcus struggled to recall it three times when briefing him, so who knows how he managed to recall it when cashing in his chips. He supposed it was just another part of his charmed demeanour: only the lucky and the stupid made it through their days unscathed. Everyone else had to revise their expectations accordingly and normally for the worse.

It wasn't like the fake ID cost much, certainly a

lot less than the total stuffed in their takeaway bags when they walked off. So, for the first time in a long time, he revised his expectations for the better. And as the evening crept in whilst they walked out, it became clear that all they needed to do was make it off Watson Street.

An electric blue strip of sky hung over their heads, a last measure of light and a rare flush of colour against the grey. He twisted his head to follow it as his legs took him up the narrow street and back towards the Hall. Marcus led him by the elbow, his eyes pointed back to the casino. They dipped down Windmill Street and he turned his head briefly to see the spot where he'd been taken off his feet by the cyclist.

Marcus led him to a barbershop at the far end of Chinatown. He sat down whilst the bearded and heavily tattooed man cut strips off his friend's scalp, rubbed fragrant oil into his beard and pretended not to be bothered by the loamy smell of the man frozen with fear in his chair. The barber asked Marcus if the work was OK. He nodded quickly and pulled thirty notes from the bag once the man looked like a wealthier, more uptight version of himself. This is who Ernest Hallenhoofer was to Marcus.

His skin buzzed and he felt every whisper the city offered on his newly exposed scalp. Marcus then took him to buy suits, shirts, shoes, underwear and socks. He deferred to his young companion as the unfamiliar sight he sometimes saw looking back in restaurant windows became an even more un-familiar one carrying a heavy burden of shopping bags. The last purchase was a walk-on flight case to store the clothes and money before they feasted on unpronounceable artisan sandwiches, feeding the crusts to the fat pigeons in Piccadilly Gardens. They placed the wrappers in the empty takeaway bags and stuffed them in a bin before walking back towards Manchester's beating heart.

The glow of the hotel leaked out of the sheltered windows and gave his companion a slightly demonic countenance in the advancing night. Marcus thought this was good. They were less likely to ask questions that way. 'You give them this when they ask for a card, yeah?'

'I have money,' the man said. His friend just shook his head.

'Nah. The only hotels that don't require plastic still charge by the hour,' Marcus replied. 'This is a classy place.' He put his hands on the man's arms and looked at him with pride. 'Remember, call reception and ask for fresh towels after seven. Make sure you give your name so I know where to find you. Oh, and don't take anything from the minibar. They charge it straight to the card, and I can't be buying no twenty-pound peanuts or even have that shit on my bill.' The man nodded. 'Seriously. My mum checks it.' The man's head gently pivoted away so he could turn his eyes to the Hall. Marcus realised that, despite appearances, the man was still the same. Anything other than the bricks, mortar and memories standing to the side of him were of little importance.

Marcus checked his watch and gave him a quick embrace. 'You've got this,' he said. The man took a deep breath and walked slowly up the steps to the front doors; his only hesitancy born of a selfish desire for the moment to stretch so far that it might never end. He walked in new shoes. The soft leather seemed to absorb his feet. His skin bathed in the glow of the foyer lights. The threads of his dark suit glistened. He felt eyes on him. He could almost hear the cycle of questions spinning through their heads. The delicate tap of his soles timed the journey to the desk: an elegant glissade that left the receptionist speechless. He had this. He was home.

5. SHEILA TAKE A BOW

LIKE MANY CELESTIAL objects that burn so brightly, Marc Bolan's light shone all too briefly. He left the earth in 1977, leaving a glimmering trail in his wake. This trail inspired some to pick up guitars, write songs and form bands. Others took his legacy and used it to sell their products, or to provide amusing names for their hotel suites (such as the one where he found himself). But that's how cultural innovation works over time: the exciting and new become normalised until the song that once rewired your brain becomes nothing more than the soundtrack to your favourite petrol advert.

Bolan himself was inspired by Bob Dylan to such an extent that he adopted a stage name that was a contraction of his hero's. So it seemed entirely fitting that this would be the destination for their test launch, the first few steps of their new experiment (too soon to call it a business – it may have been no more than a strange working holiday). The date was a winter night in 1969. Tyrannosaurus Rex would play in concert with John Peel and friends. Marcus plucked it out of his phone screen after googling 'Who is Marc Bolan?'

Unlike the boy, he knew their destination; it was only a few years after the Bob Dylan show. The fashions hadn't changed that much, and the music wouldn't have been that different either (the glitter and the glam and the plugged-in guitars would follow). His current surroundings, however, were a little more alien. The Marc Bolan suite was a small room a few floors up. The small size of the place was the first thing he noticed. Perhaps having the sky as his ceiling and the city's boundaries as his bedroom gave him an unrealistic perception of space, but in his mind the rooms would be grandiose chambers with huge ceilings and plenty of space between the walls. But, after several minutes straining with the door and the keycard, he managed to see the truth.

The carpet was the next thing he noticed. It was plaited with wavy lines that made him feel discombobulated and slightly nauseous. The deep pile absorbed his feet like it was trying to steal his shoes.

He took long soft strides across like he was gently traversing a strange planet with uncertain gravity. He moved to the window and opened the blinds to see the old brown-brick G-Mex Centre curled up on the street whilst that big new tower glowered overhead like a modern vanquisher. The windows were fixed shut, presumably to stop people throwing themselves out.

He placed his back to the glass and opened his eyes slowly to the walls. They were covered in hundreds of thin, multicoloured lines that fell horizontally and flickered like TV static. It was like they couldn't settle on one colour so agreed to include them all. His eyes hurt. The air was so thick. It was all so quiet. A flat television on a nest of mirrored drawers flicked on and tried to communicate with him. He dove on the bed and was nearly thrown back to the carpet. He reached for the phone with shaking hands and cried for fresh towels.

Their journey would only be a few floors and some fifty years, Marcus thought. Not so bad. 'So you just take the date and close your eyes?'

'I think so,' he replied. He seemed paler to Marcus. His skin was waxy and white, or whiter than normal.

His eyes kept darting to the floor like he saw something moving.

'What is it?' he asked. 'You OK? We don't have to do this.'

'We do,' he said, steadying himself with a few deep drinks of cool air that drifted from the humming unit. 'I think of the date and we go back.'

'Wait. I know a few of his records,' Marcus said.

'What?'

'Bolan. The one off that nappy ad. Glitterbug Boogie, or whatever.'

'This is before,' the man said. Deep chugs of air. *Focus. Focus.* 'He played acoustic before that.'

'Why would anyone want to see that?' Marcus asked.

The man shrugged. 'If there's not a big crowd then we find each other easier.' He then demonstrated the physical signal that would allow them to recognise one another in different bodies.

'I'm not doing that,' Marcus said, shaking his head and taking his own look at the carpet.

'All right. But if you see someone do it, walk over and say hello.'

'Not a chance.'

He looked up at Marcus, smiled and reached out his hand.

'What about what happened last time?' he asked.

'Your dad?'

'No,' Marcus said, creating a sound like that was the furthest thing from his mind. 'What if we get the same thing, it goes all scrambly.'

'That's why we need to find each other.' They'd done too much to go back. They were now at the front of the queue for the roller coaster. It was still physically possible to turn back, but far from the done thing.

So he closed his eyes and reached out his hand.

There's cold air from somewhere. Were winters in the sixties colder? Maybe doors were thinner. The hall seems familiar, though, quieter this time. They arrived early. There's a man in a body stocking doing mime onstage. He's trapped in an imaginary phone box. *Maybe 'acoustic' meant something else in the seventies? Wait. Is that David Bowie?* Marcus wonders, pondering the thin white mime onstage. Bad thoughts blow in on the breeze. He has to leave. He can't be here if his dad is. The question of whether he would travel from Moss Side in the bitter cold to watch one

153

of his future idols do mime doesn't get an airing until later. Marcus must go. He runs to the exit and through the doors just as Bowie frees himself from his invisible box.

There's a huge painted mural in the foyer; it shows people from the past screaming and running with wounded lying in the streets. Flags and smoke and turmoil. He keeps running too. He has the fear again, like the time he took acid and thought Maine Road was a giant cockroach. But he doesn't have friends to give him orange juice and explain the history of Manchester City while their faces melt. Right now he has nothing and no one. He pushes against the doors. It's all black out there.

And so cold.

Marcus opens his eyes wide. Everything is blurry. He's behind some thick glass, a small grid of numbers in front of him. The lights are bright as shit. There's rattling and thumping in the distance. Everything smells of bleach and wet biscuits. He turns his head. It's like steering a ship. The voice of God shouts, 'Queen Bee under a tree!' Closer voices sigh in response. He gets caught square in the ribs with the crook of an elbow. His bones feel like driftwood.

'Sheila! Love!' a voice says. 'Seventy-three! Love!'

'Sheila?' someone else calls. 'You all right, yer dozy cow?'

He looks down at his hands. At the liver spots and desiccated skin, the plump fingers wrapped in thin bands of gold and crowned with jewels. He looks at the bingo card, at the stamp in his hand, and the number 73 that wants to join its friends in the black inky hereafter. He turns to his friends and catches sight of himself trapped in the bright reflections of their glasses. He drops the stamper and squishes the number. A voice in his ear screams 'HOUSE!'

He screams too.

6. RUINED IN A DAY

NO HOSPITALS ARE good to wake up in, but all of them are good to leave. That was Marcus's experience. At fourteen he suffered a ruptured appendix that almost turned his skin grey. He had to wait it out on a ward with three old men. That went down to two when one of them, fed up with waiting for a doctor, forcibly discharged himself out of the window. It was the ground floor, but, still, it didn't help form good memories of places that are supposed to make you feel better.

The place he opened his eyes to was different; he had his own room with a big TV on the wall. There was a carpet on the floor. The bed felt like it had only slept him in it and, upon checking his arms and face, he realised that, yes, it *was* he that was almost enjoying it.

It was quiet, too. No shouts and echoes rolling

down stark bleached corridors, no wailing from afar. No old men showing their (literal) arses as they made a last-ditch break for freedom across the car park. The food looked all right as well, but his body wasn't ready.

'Boy.' His mum. Damp-eyed, placing a soft warm hand on his aching head. 'I was so worried about you.'

'Where are we, Mums?' he asked. A tear spilled down her cheek. 'Is it MRI?' She laughed.

'We've moved up in the world.' She plucked the tear from her cheek with a piece of tissue. 'But if there's anything else wrong we should get it checked now.' He wanted to smile, but the body was weak. 'The nice doc says we can take you home tomorrow.'

'What's the nasty one say?'

She prodded him. 'There are no nasty ones.' She gave him a kiss on the head and waved him *bye* before closing the door lightly. He didn't even hear her steps fade.

South Manchester. Trendy bars and TV stars. Aspiration should have painted the leafy suburbs around the hospital as a desirable place to live, but the thought of rubbing shoulders with the bellends he saw from the bus window seemed worse than finding himself in the body of a seventy-year-old white lady. A nervous breakdown was the layman's term for what had happened. *He had been working really hard*, his mum had said to the doctor, like he was fourteen again. Marcus suspected that, upon exiting the Free Trade Hall, he'd managed to wake up in the current incarnation of the body he was piloting back in the seventies. Poor Sheila. He was just grateful that she was alive. To do that and wake in a coffin or have your consciousness leave the stage forever didn't bear thinking about. None of this escaped his mind; he just signed the release form, was told his stay was already paid for and walked slowly to the bus stop with his mum. She wouldn't tell him how long it had been. Her eyes turned away when he asked, and she looked for something else to talk about. 'New balti house there,' she said as the bus tore down Rusholme's Curry Mile. 'How many bulbs in that sign, you reckon?'

When they got home it was the same. She'd give a running commentary on everything: TV stars, news, neighbours, the bad state of the roads, anything but the passing of time. Marcus thought about his friend. If he made it out then surely even he would have been turned off the Free Trade Hall (not to mention gently turfed out when his seven days were up). The thought of their grand business plan made him wince like there was a knife in his soul.

He'd try and get back to work once he could bring himself to think about it. Health insurance must have been covering his bills, so it's not like they'd turned their back on him completely. When he was ready he'd absorb whatever bullshit his boss threw his way, and he'd get his head down and work his way up. That was it. That was all there was to it. The scenic route to success. That would do him.

'Where you off?'

'Money never sleeps, Mums,' he said with a smile before snatching a slice of toast. He grabbed his jacket from behind the door and kissed her on the cheek. 'Want to see when I can start back.' There was a letter for him on the table. *Probably a bill, God's way of getting you back to work*, he thought. He took a deep breath and steeled himself for a long day, but something snatched his gaze on the way out.

The record player had been dormant about as long as he had. *Ziggy* stretched on it like he had no place else to go.

'Your father loved that record,' she said. Her eyes drifted off someplace. 'I did too.'

'You?' he said with more disbelief than he thought himself capable. The memory of the static crackle before the slow drum opening of 'Five Years' was matched only by the accompanying sigh that his mum would let out when it played. He had other memories, and he knew exactly at what point on the clock his mum's eyes would stop when she rolled them as Bowie observed how little time they had left. More times than not, she'd take the record off and put something else on, like The 5th Dimension or some other cosmic soul nonsense. *'But you went to see him!'* was his dad's desperate plea. *'And he was SHIT!'* was his mum's reply as they entered the 'Age of Aquarius' again.

But 'we met at a David Bowie concert,' was what she said that morning. 'The old Free Trade Hall. I knew all the words.' Her voice faded and her eyes moistened as they beheld the return of some tender memory.

Marcus felt the walls turn. He opened the envelope and saw printed numbers on a bank statement inside. His heart kicked and his stomach lurched as waves of nausea washed through him. He looked at his mum as if she could be folded away, just a prop he'd created to ease his existence.

He ran. His feet took him all the way to the city, past the brewery, the low houses and the parks, towards the tall towers and the restaurants and the hotels. He followed the fading glow of the early morning as it took his breath. He had to try and undo whatever it was they'd done. He had to find him.

Marcus's skin was dripping wet and cold. His damp shirt felt like it was mauling him. Sweat gathered in places he didn't know existed. Anyone who saw him would think he was just a casualty of the night before: a drunken, man-sized cockroach caught in the grey fridge-light of the morning. He staggered breathlessly past the crook of Oxford Road as it ran into Peter Street, past the sweet-smelling suits and the musty aimless planted outside the stark circle of the Central Library. He marched over crossings, oblivious to the angry bark of car horns and the glower of the red men. His breath fell in quick punches. He threw his last swing on the third step, collapsing outside under the arches and the awnings of the Hall. His back slid down the stone wall until he felt the cold seep into his buttocks. A silver penny pinged off the ground by his feet and rolled into the gutter. A laugh escaped him. He took a deep breath and got to his feet. It gathered on the glass doors on the return journey and slid away as he felt the warmth of the foyer on his face. He took another breath and entered the hotel. It felt a bit like coming home.

'You can't be here, Marcus.' When Krysia said his name, it sounded like 'Marcoos'. He felt a warm fuzz of nostalgia and deep shame to be presenting himself in such a sorry state. He knew there was an alternate, more officious, reading if he came back and met anyone else. Thankfully, she was his friend and seemed to work every shift God gave.

'Is he still here, Krys?' She knew who he was talking about; he saw her swallow something under her blue shirt collar. 'It's really important.' She nodded quickly, though her green eyes were fixed on the computer screen. 'Lend me your pass,' he whispered. She glanced at him: slick with sweat, breathless and possessed with some strange impassioned countenance. He looked insane but not dangerous like she'd been told. He was still gentle Marcus, still chasing the thoughts in his head, just with more conviction than she'd seen. 'Tell them I stole it,' he said. 'Let me catch a lift, then tell them.' The keycard was on the desk before he noticed. Was it here all the time, waiting for him to give it purpose? He palmed it quickly and tried to smile.

Her eyes darted to him. 'He's at the top,' she said. 'In Bob Dylan.'

Time was at your mercy in the Dylan suite. If you could afford it for the night then the day tended to arrive at your behest. All you needed to do was push a button and let the sky fall in. Marcus pushed a wet ear to the wood and rapped his knuckles lightly. It was all quiet. He looked back towards the lift and slipped the card in the lock.

He was living in a perpetual twilight, a strange hinterland between the shores of sleep and the sea of consciousness. He'd spent so much time enjoying deep dives into the past, swimming in the storied musical history of Manchester's mouthpiece that he wasn't sure if they were weeks at all. His memories were a kaleidoscopic grab bag of the old and new. Now he resided in the lavish embrace of the hotel's Bob Dylan suite.

He could feel his brain buckling under the weight of it all, but that could have been the strange modish surroundings of the new digs he was currently housed in. So strange it was, so continually unfamiliar, that he

163

wasn't sure if Marcus was emerging through the grey gloom, if he was a living invention, or a broadcast memory. He'd never seen him like now, of that much he was sure. His eyes seemed closed and guarded, his face fixed, drawn and filled with tension. The warm stirrings in his chest gave way to small flutters of panic as the boy slowly approached. Was that a white flag gripped tightly in his hand? His last reserve of optimism hoped it was a signifier of peace or a plea for surrender. It soon gave way as he saw the printed numbers on the reverse and the look on Marcus's face He rose quickly from the chair and pressed the remote. Manchester's skyline entered via the tall windows and stole the boy's attention. The tall clock tower stood face to face with Marcus whilst the rest of the city seemed to cower. 'I thought I knew Manchester till I came here,' he said, moving closer, sharing the view.

'I could say the same about you,' Marcus said. He'd never been in the penthouse; looking longingly at pics on the website was as close as he'd ever got. It offered a wide glass table buffeted by large marshmallow-like sofas around three of its edges. A large flat-screen TV imposed itself upon a large, dark wooden bureau, whilst subtle sunken rings in the ceiling provided the lighting: a deep orange glow that made everything look studious and expensive. 'What's this?' He passed the paper. The man's dark eyes narrowed and soon slid off the page, finding no meaning. 'It's a credit card bill,' Marcus said, answering his own question. 'You'll find it all comes from here.'

'I got hungry,' the man said with a shrug. He slid his feet over the soft grey carpet and slipped them into some expensive-looking cotton slippers. Then he walked over to a baby black monolith, cracked one end and released two bottles of water. 'If this is about the money, I can pay you,' he said. 'There's plenty more.'

'You're still going back? Even with what happened to me?'

The man's skin seemed to glow in the daylight as much as Marcus's seemed to be repelled by it. 'I don't know what happened to you,' he said. 'We got you to hospital. That was weeks ago.'

'You've just been sat here eating peanuts in the meantime?'

'And so much more,' he replied. There was a steely purpose in his eyes; they burned the outside reflection away. 'Not just paying your hospital bills.' The words seemed to drain some of the tension from Marcus; he could see his shoulders drift lower.

165

'We need to stop. We're not just going back there, we're changing things . . . fucking them up,' Marcus said. 'My parents met at the fair. My dad won a big pink elephant and went up to my mum to get rid of it. A few months later they were married. Isn't that a nice story? But now they met here. How messed up is that?' He clutched his head in his hands with such despair that the man was glad the human-sized windows were permanently closed. 'I don't even know if I'm the me I was any more. And what's happened to you? What's all this crap?'

He was dressed in silk pyjamas. The suits Marcus had bought him were hung on hooks in the cupboard like sides of beef in the slaughterhouse. At first he'd worn them to 'the gatherings', but the lack of actually moving anywhere and spending time in his physical form meant he favoured comfort. Besides, they gave him a slightly otherworldly, exotic quality that his visitors seemed to appreciate (at least that's what his new manager had told him).

'I was so preoccupied with the city's past that I turned from its future. What you're saying is just what I needed to hear.' The man's enunciation, his presence, had thrived in the high altitude. He possessed a confidence that Marcus had seen before, from people who weren't just unconcerned by your presence, they didn't seem to know you were there. 'We can make the future like it should be.'

Marcus shook his head and took a breath. 'At secondary school there was this quiet little kid called Tommy. He didn't speak to many kids but he seemed to like me. One day in year nine he walked up to me and told me he'd gone home and wanked into a teaspoon, normal as you might say you went home and kicked a ball. He got a scholarship to a private academy later that year. Then went into politics after Oxford. Shit, he could go and cure cancer for all I know. But no matter what he did or what he'll do there's always going to be someone out there who knows him as "Tommy Teaspoon". You see what I'm saying? You can't really change the past,' Marcus said. 'Least not with me. To me, you'll always be a man with a teaspoon.' The man kept his gaze on the city. Marcus knew his own voice would always be quieter. 'So who *are* you going back with?'

'Wait and see,' the man replied, glancing out of his suite to the clock tower while his hand pointed to the large bureau as if he hadn't heard a single word Marcus had said. 'They'll be here soon.'

*

They entered in hallowed silence.

Marcus recognised someone from *Coronation Street*, a well-heeled property developer peacocking in a shimmering tweed suit with a resigned female companion whose eyes seemed blind to the glare. A young, nervous couple followed with an old lady who looked like she didn't know where she was. They were ushered towards the sofas by the hotel manager who had the easy-going demeanour of a suicidal pall-bearer.

Marcus's boss. No. Ex-boss. The sighs and awkward, unreciprocated greetings suggested that they were gathered around the man in his silken PJs. The thin cracks of the bureau doors allowed him to see the manager take his place by the room's entrance. That was his new business partner. No wonder Marcus wasn't allowed in. The man's disapproving gaze suddenly fell on the bureau like he could read his thoughts. Marcus felt a sensation in his stomach that he hadn't felt since his school days: an invisible hand reaching down and petrifying his balls.

The manager then turned his eyes to the sofa for a few moments and, as the muttering subsided, let himself out of the room. Marcus gently slid the suits to the end of the rail and slowly stepped out of the bureau.

They were beached on the sofas like their bones had dissolved. He recognised a recent United signing in the young man. The old lady was perhaps his mum, based on the sight of his head resting on her shoulder. The young lady had her head in the other lady's lap. *Her* partner's head was angled against his shoulder. Their limbs were entangled; their bodies made a nest around the man. Manchester's brightest, best and most beautiful. Or at least its richest and most connected. Marcus heard their breathing; nothing else but the hum of the overworked air conditioning. He stepped past them and into the bedroom. There were takeaway food containers and empty bottles all over the floor. An electric guitar lay redundant on the bed. Every power socket held a plug-in air freshener. The man had been paid in cash this time and many more.

There were bags of it. He saw the notes spilling from the lips. He could take it. That's what he thought. All he had to do was pick them up and walk away. He could move out, move away with his mum. Start again, out of the city, wherever he wanted. He wouldn't be missed. He couldn't be found.

Then the thought reached him. Where were they now? Whose lives were they changing, ending, erasing? He closed the bedroom door after himself. And he walked up to the man, and he stood over him, and he grabbed his arm.

7. JUDAS

DYLAN. IT ALL came back to Dylan. He'd tried so many performances: Pink Floyd, Leonard Cohen, Skynyrd, Budgie, AC/DC, Slade – he even took requests for something more contemporary, like The Inspiring Carpets and some girl who sang a song about being made of cornflakes as the world tore itself in two. Each and every visit was plagued with technical issues: muddy visuals, squealing white noise or performances that did not warrant the high price of entry. Eventually they settled on Dylan. He was a musical icon and, for some reason (which he eventually thought might have been his real-world proximity to the venue when the performance took place), it almost always went off without a hitch.

Almost.

He hated the people he brought back: overconfident, under-intelligent, supremely entitled wankers for the most part. They would skrike about the song choices, the lack of bass in the venue, the wine list, the fact they couldn't take souvenirs or venture backstage to congratulate the young poet on his 'Nobel Peace Prize'. The complaints were eventually nipped in the bud by a thick and sturdy legal document that none of them managed to make through but all of them signed. It had the desired effect of dampening their desire to redesign the past to their own specifications. There was no more complaining once they'd signed the paper... that he could hear at least.

For his part he'd became immune to the perform-ance. Once he'd sat transfixed by the magic a small man in a grey suit could conjure with just a guitar and a harmonica. Now he just counted the minutes until he could take them back. Communing with the city had become a job. Over the dozens of visits his man-ager had scheduled, he became better at controlling the placement of their consciousness. His familiarity with the audience meant he could place a couple within a couple, a muso near the front, a heckler at the back, close friends with close friends, and so on and so forth. So impressed was his new manager that he was thinking of upscaling: using the empty Roman pool for a mass gathering, maybe filling the whole audience with paying customers.

But ennui ran deep. It started to chew on his soul. No matter how much he told himself otherwise, he was becoming a sellout, a traitor. It started to hurt. So he realised he had to do more than observe; he had to build. Like the Mancunian forefathers digging into the earth, he had to muddy his hands and set down long-lasting blocks that would be admired by generations to come.

And build he had...

It was six visits before he could pick his body. Nine before he could enter Dylan. Another five before he had the confidence to get onstage. Three before he could carry a tune. By now he reckoned he might have performed more times than Dylan himself. He was used to the routine: downstairs in the dressing room in his leather jacket. Cup of tea and a cigarette, then get changed into his suit. Someone asked if they could get him anything. He asked for guitar lessons.

Things have moved on since Marcus was away. He picks up on body signals between the new arrivals hidden in the crowd, subtle signs to identify their status as interlopers. But where is *he*? He stays sat down but he wants to shout. He wants to tear this place down.

He wonders where his band is. They were supposed to be here by now. What's keeping them? He smokes another cigarette. It's not like they're his lungs anyway. 'Stage in five,' calls a voice. He mouths the words as he hears them. He drops the ciggie in his teacup.

A single spotlight turns on. Bob Dylan walks onstage in a thick grey suit. There's loud applause. An acoustic guitar in his clutch and a harmonica strung round his neck like a brace. His fingers flick over the strings and still the claps. He sings over a gentle melody. Marcus recognises him. Maybe it's the eyes, or the manner, or the ego, but he knows it's *him* on-stage performing, and not Bob Dylan. He sees band members in the wings, security on the edges. He can't get to him. There's an impulse to do something, but he knows all too well how easy it is to make things worse just by being there. The man next to him tells his partner that he wished they'd gone to see Justin Bieber. Marcus's mind races whilst he sits and watches the show. Maybe he can catch him backstage?

*

The first half was all autopilot. The audience loved it. 'Mr Tambourine Man' goes gangbusters (even those who don't know Dylan know that one). He blew the shit out of that harmonica. But there's more. He assembles the band; they've all had their lessons, know their places. They go back onstage. More cheers. Apprehension tries to push forward; he shoos it away with his electric guitar. They tune their instruments. Open with a light blues jam. Then it kicks off.

This didn't happen. *This is all him*, Marcus thinks. *What a cunt.* He thinks back to that day on the steps. All he had to do was not invite him in. He's a vampire. So how come Marcus is the one with something lodged in his heart? He stands up, unable to bear it any more. It seems to catalyse; a wave of discontent spreads throughout the audience.

He ignores the crowd, all of them. They're just not ready, not worthy. He's going above and beyond for them. He's showing them the future. Somewhere out there, beyond the glare of the spotlight, he sees a man stand in the audience.

*

A single word seems to explode from his lungs. He sees it caught by the figure on stage. He plays the next one loud, but he's been struck, wounded.

He exits the stage. Some people clap, some boo. 'Judas!' that's what he'd said. Marcus. What an ingrate! What a betrayal! He seethes at the naysayers from backstage. The crowd filters out to the sound of the national anthem. It's over. The hall is empty except for the visitors he brought. Good. The boy wouldn't understand anyway. The visitors shout for his attention. He pretends not to hear. He lets security herd them out, following a short while after through the big doors of the hall. He glances up at a big picture of some people looking miserable in the foyer as he does. 'Goodnight, Mr Dylan,' someone says. He mumbles something in return.

Marcus leaves everything in the hotel room. The people are still sleeping. The bags of money are still there. But he's done. This place is done. He takes the stairs down and settles on the steps outside. He watches the people pass, the cars, the buses and the bikes, the dull light and the loud sounds. There's nothing else, but the city feels unfamiliar. Sirens sing in the distance. He gets to his feet and he walks. No direction. Just walking. He's looking for something new: a faint pulse, a sign of life.

An ambulance burns up Peter Street. He walks the other way. The city will tell him where to go. He knows it. It's just going to take some time.

ENCORE. NEW DAWN FADES

HE'D LIVED THE story and heard the legend: one night in Manchester he was branded a traitor for trying to bring change.

That city didn't deserve him.

Not that it mattered now; so much time seems to have passed. His body is old. His eyes are worse. The new climate suits him so much better. The new audience does too. He's sat in a primary school classroom in Calabasas. Bright light is pouring through the windows. A small plastic chair holds him captive as he tunes his guitar and clears his throat. The teachers look on in awe. The kids look unsure.

He'll play them a song to settle them down.

HOMETOWN TALES

AVAILABLE NOW FROM W&N